TOM PIPERSON'S PIG

and Other Culinary Delights

Thelma Minard

An Unusual Cookbook

by

Thelma Minard

Drawings by Patricia Minard

First published by Dog Ear Publishing
4010 W. 86th Street, Ste H
Indianapolis, IN 46268
www.dogearpublishing.net

ISBN: 978-160844-369-7

This book is printed on acid-free paper.

Printed in the United States of America

Dedicated to an excellent, though captive, quality assurance group, my children: Jim, Pete, Patricia, Anne, Mac, Barbara, and Martha.

Acknowledgments

This long-held dream would not have become a reality without the encouragement of my children. I am particularly grateful to Patricia for agreeing to do the drawings; to Anne and Patricia for their editorial comments and criticism; to Martha for recipe review; to Carol Emmet, copy editor par excellence; and to the folks at Dog Ear Publishing Company who smoothed out the final bumps in the road. Thank you, everyone!

TABLE OF CONTENTS

PREFACE

When his long career in the Navy came to an end, my husband Bob and I settled in the remote, northern section of Wilmot, New Hampshire, a rural town with a population of 923, a post office, and a small convenience store. We bought a large New England farmhouse built around 1825 with 170 acres of forest land. We had three school-age children (the youngest of our seven) and, at last, freedom to follow our whims and interests. While Bob spent his time exploring our land and its many possibilities, I was inspired to embrace the pioneer life, often forgoing the modern conveniences that had been installed by previous owners.

One of the joys of living in a rural area is the plethora of yard sales, church bazaars, and second-hand stores. All of them were great places to find old kitchen equipment and out-of-print cookbooks. Before long my kitchen walls were covered with household utensils of every description and heavy, cast iron pans so perfect for wood stove cookery. A tall bookcase was filled with cookbooks and pamphlets, some quite old and battered, others newer, all well smudged with use. I read through the cookbooks and selected recipes that allowed me to use some of those old utensils in modern ways and I absorbed a good bit of history as well. I learned to manage the heat of the big wood-burning stove and I took pride in canning and freezing the results of our extensive gardening efforts.

I discovered that many old recipes (and some newer ones, too) had titles that gave no hint of their ingredients or their place in the menu. Many came directly from England, others turned out to be regional variations of a familiar recipe. I thought what an amusing way to surprise family and friends! I would tell them that I would be serving Country Captain, White Cloud, and Joe Froggers or Black Buckle for dinner and then leave them to guess what they would be eating. After everyone recovered from the element of surprise, we would have a critical assessment. There were many delicious successes as well as some mediocre concoctions. Was this a recipe to keep or forget? The majority ruled and my collection grew; thus the genesis of this book.

A word about my choice of title: I believe, as do the editors of *The Oxford Book of Nursery Rhymes*, that Tom, the piper's son, stole a gingerbread fairing, not a live pig. Like many other nursery rhymes, "Tom, Tom the Piper's Son" is a reflection of the medieval times when it first appeared. I have included a recipe for Tom Piperson's Pig with a bit more information. I have also added anecdotal or historical information about a recipe wherever I could.

About the book itself: this is not a comprehensive listing of all the recipes with odd titles. Instead I have selected from my personal collection those recipes that I found particularly interesting or appealing. I have deliberately left out well-known ones such as Brownies and Hushpuppies. I have also decided not to include alcoholic beverages. What a wealth of odd names there!

All recipes have been tested and retested; friends and family members have helped. Most of the recipes take everyday ingredients that are already on hand or are easily obtainable. Some have been adapted to more modern terms, and I have also included a few original "receipts" for comparison. The index cross-references the main ingredients. Where possible I have given the source of a recipe and have included a bibliography, though most of the books are out of print and the pamphlets, magazines, and newspapers are long gone.

Have fun and enjoy!

TO WHET THE APPETITE

"Hors d'oeuvres present one of the best opportunities for the cook to show her skill and originality in combination and garnish." Writing in England in the middle of the Victorian Era, Isabella Beeton, in her book *Mrs. Beeton's Cookery and Household Management* makes a distinction between hors d'oeuvres and appetizers. The literal translation of *hors d'oeuvres* is "outside of the work," though as she used the phrase, it means a variety of appetizers, canapés, fruits, or salads that might be served before the main meal. These were to be served at the dining table; today we might use the term "starters".

To be a real appetizer, the food should be piquant and tantalizing. It should tease and awaken the taste buds and excite the appetite. It should send you to the table in happy anticipation of the meal to come. As the French say, "amusez la bouche" – amuse the mouth!

By and large, Europeans have tended to eschew the American cocktail hour before dinner in favor of a single glass of sherry or the like. As time becomes more and more of a premium our habits regarding pre-dinner libations are changing. Now they may range from a simple glass of wine to more elaborate cocktails, with hors d'oeuvres that might be a bowl of nuts or pretzels to an elaborate array of offerings. Somewhere in the wide variety of appetizers will be the right choice for you and your guests. Unfortunately not many of them fit the criteria of this book.

COPENHAGENS

These appetizers take a little time to prepare but they are worth the effort. The crunchiness of the water chestnuts is a pleasant compliment to the shrimp and parsley mixture, while the parsley and shrimp give flavor to the water chestnuts. Water chestnuts are the edible corms or underground bulbs of the Chinese sedge plant.

1 4-ounce can water chestnuts
1 3-ounce can tiny shrimp
1/4 cup mayonnaise
1/8 to 1/4 cup finely chopped fresh parsley
1 teaspoon lemon juice

Drain the shrimp; place in mixing bowl and mash with a table fork. Stir in the mayonnaise, parsley, and lemon juice and mix well. Drain the water chestnuts; slice each in half. Place a half teaspoon of the shrimp mixture on each water chestnut round. Makes approximately 48.

NUGGETS

These are so simple and easy to make, but they always make a hit when I serve them. Just be sure to have the cheeses at room temperature before you begin, then allow time to chill mixture again so that it will be easier to shape into balls.

2 3-ounce packages cream cheese
2 ounces crumbled blue cheese
1/4 teaspoon Worcestershire sauce
1/2 cup finely crushed potato chips

Combine cheeses and Worcestershire sauce until well blended. Chill for several hours. Shape into small balls and roll in potato chip crumbs. Makes about 30.

COSSACK'S DELIGHT

This is one of those recipes that I cut out of a newspaper. If there was a description of where the name originated, I missed it. My dictionary describes Cossacks as cavalrymen who roamed the southeastern part of Russia, perhaps as vagabonds in search of adventure. I can easily believe a Cossack might have been delighted to have his mushrooms served in this adventurous way.

1 pound button-sized mushrooms
2 tablespoons butter
2 tablespoons olive oil
1 clove garlic, peeled and crushed
1 small onion, finely chopped
1/2 teaspoon soy sauce
1/8 teaspoon each dry mustard, paprika, and seasoned salt
Dash of Worcestershire sauce
1 tablespoon flour
1 cup dairy sour cream
Salt and pepper to taste

Wash mushrooms. Heat butter and oil in Dutch oven or large frying pan with lid; add mushrooms, garlic, onion, soy sauce, and other seasonings. Cook for one to two minutes while stirring to coat mushrooms with butter and oil. Cover pan and simmer, stirring occasionally, for five minutes more. Blend flour with sour cream using rotary or electric beater until smooth. Add to the mushroom mixture and turn off the heat. Serve warm with cocktail picks.

INDIA SHAWL

The ingredients in this recipe combine an interesting mix of smooth and nubby texture with a delightful blend of sweet and tart flavors. I tore it out of a nameless magazine dated 1973. I have served this appetizer several times using mango chutney. However, recently I exchanged dried cranberries for the dates and used cranberry chutney instead of the sweeter mango chutney, which turned out to be a very successful substitution.

1 8-ounce package cream cheese
1/2 cup crumbled blue cheese
1/4 cup finely chopped dates [or dried cranberries]
1/4 cup finely chopped mango chutney [or cranberry chutney]
1 tablespoon lemon juice
1/2 cup finely chopped walnuts

Beat softened cream cheese with electric beater until fluffy. Add blue cheese, dates, chutney, and lemon juice and mix thoroughly. Add nuts. Mound up in serving dish. Serve with crackers. Makes about 2 cups.

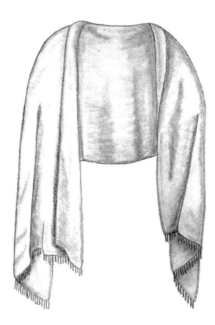

ANGELS IN ORBIT

These are quick and easy to make if you happen to have salami and oysters on hand. No quantities are given – you can make as many or as few as you wish.

For each angel place a thin slice of salami on a moderately hot griddle and fry until it curls up into a cup. Remove from heat and put a well-rinsed raw oyster in the cup. Serve hot or cold or somewhere in between.

If you would prefer DEVILS AFOOT just wrap half slices of bacon around the oysters, fasten with toothpicks, and bake at 350° for 30 minutes.

HARLEQUINS

This recipe takes extra time to prepare, but the result is a colorful presentation and a tasty variation on an old theme.

1 large cooked carrot
1 small cooked beet
12 cooked string beans
3 or 4 tablespoons mayonnaise
1/8 teaspoon salt
Pepper to taste
6 hard-boiled eggs, peeled
Paprika

Chop vegetables as finely as you can. Mix together with mayonnaise, salt, and pepper. Mixture will be a lovely shade of purple! Cut peeled eggs in half lengthwise; remove yolks and press through a sieve. Fill each half with a spoonful of the vegetable mixture and sprinkle with egg yolk. Top with a dusting of paprika. Makes 12 servings.

Leftover vegetable mixture may be served on plain crackers.

WRAPAROUNDS

Once again we have the lowly water chestnut coming to the fore. These are tasty morsels that may whet a thirst as well as the appetite due to the salt in both soy sauce and bacon. I suggest using low-sodium soy sauce to cut the amount of salt.

1/4 cup soy sauce
2 tablespoons sugar
2 small cans water chestnuts
10-12 slices bacon

Combine soy sauce and sugar. Marinate the drained water chestnuts in the soy sauce mixture for 30 minutes, turning or stirring occasionally. Cut bacon slices in half crosswise and wrap a half slice around a water chestnut. Fasten with a toothpick. Place on a rack in a shallow pan and bake at 350° for 30-35 minutes or until bacon is nicely crisped. Serve hot. Makes 20-24.

SERVED FROM A TUREEN

People have been enjoying soup ever since the discovery of fire and the use of some sort of container to hold liquid. The earliest soup "pot" was probably a large mollusk or a turtle shell, with the soup itself being made from the less meaty portions of the animal. An animal stomach was another type of container: filled with water, bits of meat, and possibly a few potherbs, the whole was tied up and hung over the fire. Much later in time, with the discovery first of clay pots and then of iron and other metals, man was on his way to the creation of myriad glorious soups.

During the Middle Ages peasant families probably subsisted almost entirely on the contents of a cauldron hung over the fire that provided a continuous but ever-changing meal with the flavor and texture being altered from day to day, week to week, by the available ingredients. It was a true *pot-au-feu.*

As the art of cooking became more refined and a greater number of foodstuffs became more readily available, soup took its place as a carefully selected and specially prepared first course. From the sixteenth century on, no proper dinner was served without one or more soups to tease the appetite. The number of *sops* served with the soup was an important indicator of the degree of hospitality being offered. A sop is anything that could be used to soak up the broth: a piece of bread or a roll, a bit of potato, or a dumpling. The more of these that were served, the more welcome a person felt.

NYMPH AURORA

This recipe is from the 1934 edition of Fannie Farmer's *Boston Cooking School Cookbook*. The name attracted my attention and, as I am very fond of shrimp, I had to try it. Pleasantly satisfied I found the soup to be light and tasty and suitable as a first course to any dinner, gourmet or otherwise. Of course in the directions you were expected to use fresh shrimp and wash, shell, devein, and cut them into small pieces. With today's convenience packaging, it is a timesaver to use canned shrimp. I added the diced celery.

1 quart chicken stock
1/4 cup finely diced onion
1/4 cup finely diced carrot
1/4 cup finely diced celery
A few good sprinkles of marjoram, mace, and thyme
2 tablespoons cornstarch
1 tablespoon lemon juice
1 can baby shrimp OR
1/2 pound raw shrimp, washed, shelled, deveined, and cut in pieces

Remove shrimp from can if using them; rinse well to remove excess salt and set aside to drain. In a small bowl combine cornstarch with a small amount of the stock; stir well to remove all lumps. Cook diced onion, carrot, celery, and herbs in the chicken stock until tender. Add the lemon juice and stir in the cornstarch mixture. Add shrimp cut in small pieces. Simmer and stir just long enough to heat the shrimp. Fannie Farmer suggested garnishing each serving with whipped cream. I do not. Makes 4 servings.

PEASE PORRIDGE

Pease porridge hot,
Pease porridge cold,
Pease porridge in the pot
Nine days old.

I can't imagine anyone who would like his pease porridge after it had stood in the pot for nine days, but the flavors are improved if they are allowed to blend for a day or two. Perhaps this is one reason that pease porridge found a regular place on the Sunday tables in Shaker communities. Their strict observance of the Sabbath precluded any unnecessary cooking and this recipe could well be made up the day before.

The word *porridge* is a form of *pottage,* meaning a food made by boiling any meat or vegetable in milk or water. If we use it at all today, we associate *porridge* with oatmeal and call pease porridge by the more specific title of Split Pea Soup. My father, known to his grandchildren as Papa Joe, developed this recipe which has long been a favorite in our family. Allow two days to prepare it.

1 hambone
1 pound split peas
2 large onions
4 carrots
2 stalks celery
1 1/2 tablespoons dried parsley
1/2 teaspoon dried marjoram
1/2 teaspoon dried thyme
Salt and pepper to taste
1 cup diced leftover ham, optional

Boil a hambone in 4 quarts of water for several hours to make a good stock. Strain into large container and set aside to allow the fat to rise to the top. Next day, skim off as much fat as you can. Now you are ready to make the soup. Rinse the split peas in a colander, checking for and removing any extraneous matter. Heat stock in large pot; add the peas, diced onions, carrots, and celery, and the seasonings. Simmer gently, stirring occasionally. If you have leftover ham add that also, then continue cooking until the peas are very mushy. As soup thickens it must be watched to prevent burning. I do not strain it. This will make 6 to 8 hearty servings.

MULLIGATAWNY

This hearty soup originated in India. There, it was called *pepper pot* and the list of the many ingredients in a true mulligatawny testifies to its spiciness. First enjoyed by British colonials of the East India Company, the recipe was brought back to England and from there easily spread among the colonies. It is particularly popular in Australia. The word, *mulligatawny,* is an anglicized translation of the Tamil words for pepper water.

Typically, the recipe was altered and modified through the years. This one is adapted from *The American Heritage Cookbook.* Originally a whole chicken would have been used, making it necessary for the housewife to spend time cleaning it and cutting it up. With the prepackaged meats that we have today cooking is not the all-consuming chore that it once was. We can even get boneless, skinless pieces of chicken that eliminate a big step in making this soup. Granny Smith apples work well in this recipe.

3 pounds chicken, cut in pieces
3 tablespoons butter
1/2 cup chopped carrots
1/2 cup chopped sweet pepper
2 green apples, peeled and chopped
1 tablespoon flour
1 teaspoon curry powder or more
2 quarts chicken broth
2 whole cloves
1/8 teaspoon mace
1 tablespoon dried parsley
1 1/2 tablespoons sugar
Salt and pepper to taste

Brown chicken pieces in butter in Dutch oven or similar pot. Stir in the carrot, pepper, and apple pieces and cook, stirring often, until mixture is brown. Stir in the flour and curry powder and then add broth gradually while continuing to stir. Season with the remaining ingredients. Bring to a boil, then reduce heat and simmer slowly until chicken is tender. If you used a whole chicken, remove the pieces from the pot and set aside until cool enough to handle, then discard skin and bones and return meat to the pot. Reheat and serve with a sturdy white bread for dunking. Serves 6 to 8.

Note: You may want to remove the whole cloves – if you can find them – or offer a prize at table for the person who finds one in his or her soup. They are not pleasant to bite on.

BLACK FROST

This recipe is adapted from one in a privately printed, fund-raiser cook book that I picked up in a secondhand store. As I scanned several pages of cold soup recipes, I was immediately reminded of my teenage years when my mother tried to introduce our family to a "new" fad: cold soup. My father would have no part of it; he was adamant that soup should always be hot and the hotter, the better. I tried it, reluctantly, but soon learned to like the idea of a nourishing cold soup for a hot summer's day. I recommend it.

1 can condensed black bean soup
1 can condensed consommé
1 soup can water
2 teaspoons sherry (optional)
Sour cream

Stir black bean soup in a medium pot; add the consommé, water, and sherry. Heat, stirring occasionally, until thoroughly blended. Allow to cool, then refrigerate for at least 6 hours. Serve in cold bowls with an ample tea-spoonful of sour cream dolloped on each serving. Serves 4.

If you prefer to make the soup yourself instead of opening the cans, here is the recipe.

1 tablespoon olive oil
1 large onion, finely chopped
3 cloves garlic, finely chopped
4 1-pound cans black beans
Juice of 1/2 lemon
1/2 teaspoon ground cumin
1/2 teaspoon dried oregano
2 tablespoons parsley finely chopped
Salt and pepper to taste
4 cups water or beef stock

Sauté onion and garlic in olive oil until translucent and soft. Combine all ingredients and simmer gently until beans can be mashed easily and onion and garlic bits have dissipated. The soup may be served at once with a dollop of sour cream and a sprig of parsley for garnish. For cold soup: cool, then chill thoroughly in refrigerator. This recipe will serve 6 to 8.

MOM'S ILLUSIONS

I'm not sure whose Mom developed this recipe. I found it in the middle of a newspaper page of recipes. It is a basic recipe that can be made ahead of time and stored on the pantry shelf. Then, when you have a sudden urge for soup, just add water and whatever main ingredient(s) you have on hand. The variety is endless.

2 cups nonfat dried milk powder
2 tablespoons dried onion flakes
4 tablespoons cornstarch
4 tablespoons chicken bouillon powder
1 teaspoon dried basil
1 teaspoon dried thyme
1/4 teaspoon black pepper
Salt to taste

Mix all ingredients together and store in an airtight container. When it is time for soup, add 2 cups water to 1 1/2 cups mix in a large saucepan. Heat over medium heat stirring constantly, until soup thickens. Add 1 to 2 cups diced, cooked leftovers and cook a few minutes longer. Voila! Two or more cups of delicious, fat-free, "cream" soup!

GALLIMAUFRIES AND HOTCHPOTCHES: SUBSTANTIAL FARE

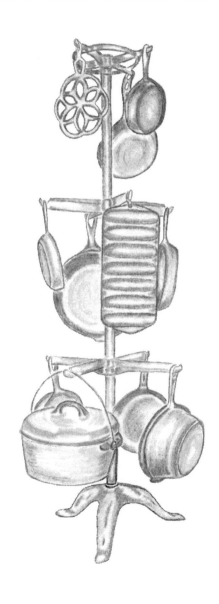

By now you must have a good idea that I enjoyed living in that old farm-house in New Hampshire and cooking on a big old wood-burning stove. With a crane still mounted in the fireplace, I could have done open-hearth cooking too, if I had really wanted to emulate a pioneer woman, but I chose not to. The stove and all the wonderful cast iron pots, pans, skillets, and griddles that I collected were enough for me.

Iron is one of the most widely spread metals in the world and the ore has been refined since ancient times. Other metals were known and used – copper, tin, lead, and their alloys – but none could withstand the direct heat of the fire as iron could. Before the early part of the nineteenth century all food except that which was baked in ovens was cooked by the direct heat of flames or coals. Cast iron was well suited to the hard usage to which it was put. Its toughness lent itself well to high heat; its even heat distribution and lasting retention of heat made it desirable for long, slow cooking; and its imperviousness to anything but the strongest acid meant it could be used in many different ways. A well-seasoned or "sweetened" utensil was easy to clean, without the labor of polishing.

I can hear the complaints: cast iron is so heavy; it tends to rust if left unused; and it is so old-fashioned. Yes, it is heavy; it won't rust if it is used with some regularity; and it may be old-fashioned, but a cast iron pot is still the best utensil for cooking a *gallimaufry*, a medley of meat and vegetables, or a *hotch-potch*, a hodge-podge of ingredients. Whether it was soup or stew or a combination of both – stoup or stewp – all winter long there would be a pot at the back of my wood-burning stove simmering away and emitting the most enticing aromas.

KENTUCKY BURGOO

There are probably more recipes, and variations of recipes, for fixing chicken than any other food we eat. Many of them have fancy French names and are in the gourmet class, using expensive or hard-to-find ingredients, but there are also many good recipes for chicken stew, albeit known by other terms, that have come down to us from the early days of American settlement. Kentucky Burgoo and Country Captain are two such recipes. They are both worth having on file to provide a change from the ever-popular and reiterative fried chicken.

Burgoo was originally thick oatmeal porridge, particularly associated with sea-faring men who apparently subsisted on it for months at a time. Taken inland, this dish soon became a staple one-pot meal during the frontier days in Kentucky where it was thickened further by the addition of meats of all kinds - squirrel, rabbit, beef, chicken - and vegetables, while the oatmeal was omitted. 'Tis thus that recipes change through the years! Burgoo today means thick stew. The recipe given here combines several that I have at hand. It will make 10 or more generous servings; however, leftovers can be frozen for another day. Since so many ingredients are involved, it makes sense to cook a quantity large enough for several meals.

1 pound lean beef, cubed
1 large soup bone
1/2 pound veal, cubed
1 chicken, cut in serving-sized pieces
3 tablespoons bacon fat
2 quarts water
1 teaspoon salt
2 tablespoons brown sugar
Spice bag containing 2 bay leaves, 4 whole cloves, 6 peppercorns, and
1/4 teaspoon crushed hot peppers
2 cups chopped onions
2 cups potatoes, peeled and diced
1 cup carrots, diced
1 cup celery, diced
1 large can tomatoes (20 ounces or more)
1 large green pepper, chopped
1 teaspoon garlic salt
1 cup fresh or frozen butter beans
1 cup fresh or frozen corn
2 cups fresh cabbage, chopped
1/2 cup chopped parsley

Heat bacon fat in large heavy pot and brown beef, veal, and chicken pieces. Add soup bone, water, salt, brown sugar, and spice bag and simmer until meat is tender. Remove chicken from kettle and when cool discard bones and skin, returning meat, to the pot. Add onions, potatoes, carrots, celery, tomatoes, green pepper, and garlic salt. If fresh butter beans are used, add them also. Simmer gently for 1 1/2 hours, stirring occasionally. Then add corn and cabbage (and frozen butter beans, if they are your choice). Continue cooking 15 to 20 minutes until these vegetables are cooked. Just before serving sprinkle with chopped parsley. Serve in soup plates, with slices of hot corn bread or crusty sourdough bread. Serves 6 to 8 several times.

COUNTRY CAPTAIN

Country Captain is presumably of East Indian origin, although Savannah, Georgia, claims it as its own. Undoubtedly a sea captain, plying the spice trade route, was responsible for introducing it to southern cooks. Its special ingredient is curry powder, a somewhat misunderstood blending of many spices and herbs. Formulas for curry powder are carefully guarded family secrets in India and may include from five to fifty different ingredients from allspice to zeodary root, from the common spices found on your kitchen shelf to exotic, unfamiliar ones. Those who have made a study of Indian food say that Americans really know nothing about curry, and I am sure they are right. I am among the know-nothings. I use what McCormick, Durkee, and Spice Islands have to offer and proceed from there, in blissful ignorance, to make and enjoy Country Captain.

One 2 1/2-pound chicken, cut in serving-sized pieces
1/2 cup flour
1/2 teaspoon salt
1/4 teaspoon pepper
3 tablespoons vegetable oil
1 medium onion, chopped
1 medium green pepper, chopped
1/2 teaspoon garlic salt
1 to 2 teaspoons curry powder
1/2 teaspoon powdered thyme
1 large can tomatoes (20-ounces or more)
1/2 cup raisins or dried currants
Toasted, slivered almonds
Cooked rice

Combine flour, salt, and pepper and dredge chicken pieces with the mixture. Heat oil in large pot and brown chicken on all sides; remove and set aside. If necessary, add a bit more oil to pot, then sauté onion and pepper. Add garlic salt, curry powder, and thyme. Scrape bottom and sides of pot to loosen all browned bits. Stir in tomatoes, then return chicken to pot. Cook slowly for 30 to 45 minutes until chicken is tender. A few minutes before serving, stir in raisins or currants. Serve over rice, garnished with almonds. Serves 4 to 6.

To toast almonds, spread in shallow pan and heat in slow oven (250°) for 15 to 20 minutes. Stir several times to brown evenly.

BIRDS, OLIVES, and ROLLS

These are all names for stuffed, rolled, and tied meat slices served with gravy. Any cooked or raw meat that can be sliced into thin pieces about 2 1/2 inches by 4 inches can be used. I found many recipes in my older cookbooks that were essentially the same; only the ingredients in the *forcemeat* (stuffing) and the gravy or sauce differed. Make the forcemeat first. You can use your own favorite recipe or this one.

Thinly sliced beef, veal, pork, lamb or chicken
1/2 medium onion
1 stalk celery
2 tablespoons butter
2 cups herb-seasoned stuffing mix
1 egg, well-beaten
water

Sauté onion and celery, both finely diced, in 2 tablespoons butter. When softened add to herb-seasoned stuffing mix along with the egg and just enough water to hold mixture together.

If necessary, pound meat slices to flatten and shape them before placing a spoonful of forcemeat in the center of each. Roll up and tie with string. If the meat is already cooked, place rolls in pan, cover with thin gravy or tomato sauce and heat through.

When using raw meat, I suggest you first brown the rolls in butter, then remove them to a baking pan, cover with sauce or broth, and cover the pan with a lid or foil. Bake at 350° for 40 to 45 minutes or until meat is cooked. This forcemeat recipe will be ample for 8 or more rolls.

SCOTCH COLLOPS

From the *Willamsburg Art of Cookery:*

"Take veal, cut it thin, beat it well with a rolling pin & grate some nut megs over them, dip them in the yolk of an egg, & fry them in a little butter until they are a delicate fine brown then pour the butter from them, & have ready a pint of gravy, a little piece of butter rolled in flour, a glass of white wine, the yolk of an egg & and a little cream mixed together. Stir it all together and when it is of a fine thickness dish it up. It does well without cream if you have none & very well without gravy, only put in just as much warm water & either red or white wine."

This recipe is not as confusing as it seems if you realize that the second half gives directions for making the gravy even though it is part of the first long sentence. *Collops* is an old English word for a thin slice of meat.

1 1/2 pounds thinly sliced veal
Ground nutmeg to taste
1 egg yolk, beaten
4 tablespoons butter, divided
2 tablespoons flour
1/2 cup milk or cream
1 egg yolk
1/2 cup white wine
1 cup water

Cut veal into six pieces. Pound each piece until it is very thin, sprinkle with nutmeg, dip in the beaten egg yolk, and sauté in 2 tablespoons butter until golden brown on each side. Remove meat from pan. Put in remaining 2 table-spoons butter, stir in flour and the second egg yolk which has been mixed with milk or cream. Continue stirring and cooking while adding wine and water until gravy is "of a fine thickness." Reheat the veal in the gravy if necessary. Serves 6.

BLIND DUCK

Mrs. Allen's recipe for Blind Duck in her 1917 *Modern Method* cookbook calls for a stuffing of onions and potatoes mixed together. However, I prefer to keep the potatoes separate so offer here my own stuffing recipe. I had been serving this to my family for years before I knew it was called Blind Duck.

1 large or 2 small flank steaks
1 medium onion
1 stalk celery
1 small can chopped mushrooms
1/2 cup herb-seasoned stuffing mix
Garlic salt, lemon pepper
Thyme
Salt and pepper to taste
String for tying

If you can find a flank steak large enough to be rolled up, you are in luck; otherwise use two smaller ones with the stuffing layered between them sandwich style. Score steaks with diagonal crisscrossing, being careful not to cut all the way through. Sprinkle both sides with garlic salt and lemon pepper.

Chop onion and celery and sauté in small amount of butter or olive oil until onion is soft. Remove pan from heat; add the stuffing mix and the mushrooms with their liquid. Add a dash or two of thyme and salt and pepper as desired. Stir to blend well. Lightly grease the bottom of a baking dish. Place stuffing on a large flank steak and roll up as for jelly roll and tie with string; or place one smaller flank steak in pan, cover with stuffing, and place second steak on top. Cover all loosely with aluminum foil and bake at 350° for 45 minutes. Serves 4 to 6 depending on the size of the steak.

PORCUPINES

These Porcupines are a nice change from the ubiquitous spaghetti and meatballs. The recipe, with my own variations, is from a book of favorite recipes compiled by folks at Memorial Hospital in Ormond Beach, Florida.

1 1/2 pounds lean ground beef
1/4 cup chopped onion
1/2 cup long-grain rice, uncooked
2 eggs
1/8 teaspoon salt
1/8 teaspoon paprika
2 8-ounce cans tomato sauce
1 tablespoon oil or fat for browning

Combine all ingredients except tomato sauce and form mixture into balls. Brown them quickly in the oil or fat, then transfer them to a heavy pot with lid. Pour the tomato sauce over all. Cover the pot and simmer for about 45 minutes. Kernels of cooked rice should be poking out giving the illusion of porcupine quills. Serves 6.

POLISH RED BARON

This hearty one-pot meal can be made ahead of time and reheated before serving. It is best served on a cold winter's night with plenty of dark bread to soak up the juices. In New Hampshire after a day of skiing or sledding, it was a satisfying meal for cold, hungry folks.

1/4 cup butter
2 medium onions, chopped
2 pounds red cabbage, shredded
4 cups tart apples, diced
1/4 cup red wine vinegar
1/4 cup water
1 tablespoon sugar
1 bay leaf
1/4 teaspoon allspice
Salt and pepper to taste
1/3 cup red currant jelly
1 1/2 pounds fully cooked Kielbasa (Polish sausage), cut in 1 inch pieces

Melt butter in a Dutch oven. Add onions and sauté until tender. Add cabbage, apples, and next five ingredients with salt and pepper as desired. Cover and cook over medium heat for one hour, stirring occasionally. Stir in the jelly and cook fifteen minutes more. Add the sausage and cook for 15 to 20 minutes more until sausage is heated through. Serve with boiled potatoes.
Makes 6 to 8 large servings.

SWISS BLISS

I suppose I could have made up a story about a fair Miss from Switzerland who created this recipe for Swiss Bliss because she wanted to get out of the kitchen and join in the fun. Instead I will admit to cutting the recipe out of a friend's magazine because I liked the sound of it. Quick and easy to prepare, the recipe makes good use of a less expensive cut of meat. The long cooking renders the steak tender and flavorful.

2 pounds chuck steak, 1 inch thick
1 envelope onion soup mix
1/2 pound mushrooms, sliced
1/2 green pepper, diced
1 16-ounce can diced tomatoes
1 tablespoon steak sauce
1 1/2 tablespoons cornstarch

Drain tomatoes, reserving juice. Cut steak into serving-sized pieces and place in lightly greased baking dish. Sprinkle with onion soup mix, and then add mushrooms, green pepper, and drained tomatoes. Combine the juice from the tomatoes with steak sauce and stir into the cornstarch, mixing well to prevent lumps. Pour over meat and vegetables. Cover tightly with lid or aluminum foil and bake for 2 hours in a 350° oven. Serves 6 to 8.

OXFORD JOHN

Roast leg of lamb was a favorite in our home, though it was usually reserved for special occasions. I found this recipe in a magazine in my doctor's office and was intrigued by the different seasonings: mace, thyme, and lemon juice. It is a delicious way to serve leftover lamb.

Thin slices of cold, roast lamb
4 tablespoons butter
3-4 tablespoons finely chopped onion
2 tablespoons flour
Pinch of salt, dash of pepper
Generous pinches of mace and thyme
2 cups stock, chicken or vegetable
Juice of half a lemon

Sauté the chopped onion in 3 tablespoons of butter until softened and golden. Sprinkle on the flour, salt, pepper, mace, and thyme and stir to blend. Gradually add the stock, stirring constantly until smooth and simmering. Add the lemon juice and the remaining butter. Place slices of meat in gravy and allow to simmer over low heat just until meat is warmed through.

SLOWGLOW

This is another of those recipes that does so well with slow cooking for a longer period of time. To serve more or less than four, use one pork chop for each person and alter the vegetables proportionately.

4 lean pork chops, about 1 1/2 inches thick
2 small sweet potatoes
2 small white potatoes
4 carrots
4 stalks celery
1 large onion
1 6-ounce can tomato paste, diluted with
3 cans water

Trim fat from chops. Scrub potatoes and leaving skin on, cut into bite-sized pieces; cut carrots and celery in the same way. Place vegetables in large casserole or Dutch oven, lay meat on top. Slice onion and lay on top of meat. Dilute tomato paste with water and pour over all. Cover dish and bake at 325° for one hour or until vegetables are done and the meat is tender. Serves 4.

Note: My vegetarian daughter said this was excellent with kidney beans substituted for the pork chops.

PIGS-IN-BLANKETS

There are many different recipes for Pigs-in-Blankets. Some call for sausages or oysters wrapped in bacon and then fried or baked and served as an appetizer. This particular one has more ingredients and takes more time to make, but it is filling and delicious, and definitely fits the descriptive title. Youngsters love this dish, but I think it's the name that really intrigues them.

1 package frankfurters
1 teaspoon minced onion
1 teaspoon minced parsley
2 cups mashed potato
2 eggs
1 tablespoon water
Fine bread crumbs
Vegetable oil or shortening for frying

Cut frankfurters in half, heat through in simmering water. Combine minced onion, parsley, potato, and one egg and mix well. Coat each frankfurter piece with potato mixture then roll in crumbs, dip in second egg which has been stirred with 1 tablespoon water, than roll in crumbs again. Heat about 1 inch of oil or shortening in frying pan; fry Pigs-in-Blankets until golden brown. Drain on absorbent paper. Serves 6.

THE SULTAN'S FAVORITE

This is a great way to use leftover chicken or turkey. The original recipe from my grandmother's recipe book gave directions for boiling a fowl in water with celery and onion. When it was cooked, she removed the meat from the bones, strained the liquid, and cooled it to let the fat rise to the top. With prepackaged and prepared foods in stores these days we can eliminate much of the work.

3 cups cooked chicken or turkey
1 pound asparagus, cooked
6 tablespoons butter
1/2 cup flour
1 cup milk
2 cups chicken broth
1 cup mayonnaise
1 teaspoon lemon juice
1/2 teaspoon curry powder
Salt and pepper to taste
Pimiento

Melt butter in saucepan, blend in the flour, and gradually add milk and broth. Cook over low heat until thick and smooth, stirring constantly. Remove from heat and add mayonnaise, lemon juice, and curry powder; then beat with a rotary beater until all lumps are removed.

Arrange half the cooked asparagus in bottom of a two-quart baking dish, place chunks of chicken or turkey on top, arrange remaining asparagus on top of the meat, and pour the sauce over all. Garnish with thin slivers of pimiento. Bake in a 400° oven for 20 minutes or until heated through. Serve with rice to 6 or 8.

LOBSCOUSE

Originally a stew of fat and hardtack with a dash of vinegar, lobscouse or *skillygolee* was a frequently served dish in the galleys of New England whaling ships. Along with *salt horse* (dried, salted corned beef), *long lick* (a molasses drink), and *dandy funk* (a dessert of powdered hardtack and molasses), it was rugged fare. This modernized version can be made well ahead of time and allowed to simmer slowly all day or, as this recipe suggests, boil for an hour, and then simmer a short time.

1 1/2 pounds bottom round beef
4 cups raw potatoes
1/2 pound salt pork
4 onions
4 cups cooked corned beef

Cut bottom round, peeled potatoes, and salt pork into small cubes. Place in large pot. Peel onions and cut in small chunks; add to pot. Cover with water and boil with lid on pot for one hour. Add the cut-up corned beef and simmer for 1/2 hour. Serves 6 to 8 hungry sailors.

JOHNNIE PESUKY

This recipe comes from Volume IV of *Favorite Recipes of America*. There is no indication of how it got its name or where in America it came from. No matter, it is an easy dish to put together, tastes good, and if you are lucky enough to have leftovers, it reheats very easily and tastes even better than the day before.

2 tablespoons olive oil
1/2 medium onion, diced
1/2 medium red pepper, diced
1 cup diced cooked pork or ham
1 cup elbow macaroni, uncooked
1/2 cup grated cheddar cheese
1 18-ounce can tomato/basil soup plus
1/2 cup water to rinse can
1 14.5-ounce can diced tomatoes and juice
1 small can mushroom bits and juice
Salt and pepper to taste

Sauté onion and red pepper in the olive oil until soft. Combine all ingredients in buttered casserole. Cover tightly and bake in a 375° oven for one hour or until macaroni is cooked and some of the liquid has been absorbed. Serve in soup plates with hot crusty bread. Serves 6.

KEDGEREE

This fish and rice dish originally came from India where it was a highly spiced food, usually made with lentils, and served with curry. During the time of the East India trade, English sea captains brought the recipe back to England where it quickly became a popular breakfast dish. Gradually, through the years, the spices and lentils have been left out and, in this country, kedgeree is served for lunch or dinner rather than at breakfast time. The best recipe I have found for kedgeree is in the Gourmet Cookbook but it is very time consuming. Mrs. Beeton in *Cookery and Household Management* offers an easier version. I added the onion and herbs.

2 tablespoons olive oil
1/2 cup chopped onion
2 cups cooked, flaked fish
1 cup cooked rice
2 hard-boiled eggs, peeled
1/8 teaspoon of your favorite dried herb (thyme, basil, oregano, etc.)
Fresh parsley for garnish

Cut eggs in half lengthwise and remove the yolks. Slice whites of eggs; sieve the yolks and set aside. Heat olive oil in flat pan, add all ingredients except the egg yolks; stir and cook until just heated through. Turn into serving dish, garnish with the sieved yolks and small sprigs of parsley. Serves 6.

Mrs. Beeton, writing in the mid-19th century, also gave this recipe for Indian Kedgeree. I include it just for interest. Ghee is clarified butter; dhall is made from lentils.

INDIAN KEDGEREE

4 ounces onions
4 ounces ghee
4 ounces dhall
4 ounces rice
Stock or water
Peppercorns, cloves, cardamoms, cinnamon, salt, green ginger

Heat ghee, fry sliced onion until brown. Remove onion. Add dhall to ghee in pan, also rice, cook until ghee is absorbed, then barely cover with stock or water; add spices. Cook gently until quite dry. Garnish with onion. Serves 4.

MEDITERRANEAN SAUTÉ

I found this recipe by chance when I was waiting in a train station and picked up a section of newspaper for something to read. It sounded so good that I tore it out with the idea of stopping for the ingredients on my way home. As happens, the store did not have scallops for sale that day, but I have served this several times since and it is always well received.

1 tablespoon olive oil
1/2 pound sea scallops
1/2 cup red onion, chopped
1 red bell pepper, chopped
1 yellow bell pepper, chopped
6 to 8 asparagus spears, cut in small pieces
1 pound fettucine
6 sprigs cilantro, chopped
Salt and pepper to taste

Sauté the scallops in olive oil in a large pan over medium heat until they become translucent and firm, but not chewy (about 5 minutes). Remove from pan and set aside, covered. In the same pan, sauté the red onion and the peppers, cook for 5 to 7 minutes, then add the asparagus pieces and cook for 2 minutes more.

Meanwhile cook the fettucine by package directions to the *al dente* stage. Drain and transfer to a serving dish.

To the vegetables in the skillet add the scallops and cilantro. Cook and stir just enough to reheat the scallops. Spoon the mixture over the fettucine and serve with a salad of mixed greens and some crusty hot bread for a hearty meal. Serves 6.

STUFFED TURBANS

This recipe is adapted from Fannie Farmer's *The Boston Cooking School Cook Book.* It works best with flounder, which seems to have a symbiotic relationship with crabmeat.

1 pound flat fish filets (sole, flounder, or tilapia)
3/4 cup chopped mushrooms
1/4 cup chopped onion
3 tablespoons butter
4 1/2 tablespoons flour
1/2 cup cream
1/2 cup crab meat OR 12 oysters, chopped
Salt and pepper to taste
Buttered bread crumbs

Trim filets, and then line the insides of well-buttered muffin tins with them. Cook mushrooms and onion, in butter; add flour, stir well, then add cream gradually, stirring constantly. Bring to boil, add crabmeat or oysters, season to taste. Fill muffin tins with mixture, cover with foil, and bake 20 minutes at 375°. Sprinkle with buttered bread crumbs and return to oven till brown. Serves 4 to 6.

THE CORONADO CREATION

This was a favorite dish with Navy wives in Coronado, California. No one seems to know who first put it together or if it ever had a proper name. We just called it the Creation. It was well established as luncheon fare by the time I was introduced to it. I copied the recipe from a friend's notebook just as she had copied it from her friend.

1 large green pepper, chopped
1 medium onion, chopped
3 or 4 stalks celery, chopped
1 6 1/2-ounce can crab meat
1 6 1/2-ounce can shrimp
1 teaspoon Worcestershire sauce
1 cup mayonnaise
1 small can water chestnuts, cut in pieces
1 small can sliced mushrooms
Salt and pepper to taste
Soft bread crumbs
Butter or margarine
Paprika
Lemon wedges

In a large bowl combine all but the last four ingredients and stir so that they are well blended. Place in a buttered casserole dish, top with the bread crumbs, dot with butter, add a sprinkling of paprika, and bake at 350° for 30 minutes or until heated through and bubbly. Garnish with lemon wedges. Serves to 4 to 6.

Note: Water chestnuts are pieces of the edible corm (underground stem) of Chinese sedge. Their crispness adds a great deal to the texture of this dish.

JANSSEN'S TEMPTATION

Eric Janssen came to America from Sweden in the mid-1840s with a group of religious dissenters whom he led into Henry County, Illinois. Under his tireless direction they cleared the land, planted wheat and corn, and built a cross-shaped tabernacle large enough for 1,000 people. The new town was named Bishop Hill and by 1850 he had recruited many more followers. Like the Shakers, he believed that God was best served by the people who lived in isolated communities and were devoted to doing His work. He preached self-denial in all things and, as with the Shakers, it was the philosophy of celibacy that caused the disintegration of his community. Janssen was killed by John Root, a young man in love with his niece.

Apparently, Janssen did not practice everything he preached, for the story goes that one day one of his people came upon him sitting alone feasting secretly on a dish of potatoes and anchovies that had been cooked in milk and butter. Evidently the yearnings of his youth in Sweden had welled up in him so strongly that he was tempted to sample once again this dish that is, I believe, still popular on Swedish tables.

3 to 4 medium-sized potatoes
2 2-ounce cans flat anchovy filets
1 medium onion, chopped
4 tablespoon butter
2 cups milk
1/2 cup dry bread crumbs

Peel potatoes and slice in 1/8 inch pieces. Sauté onion in three table-spoons butter; add well-drained and chopped anchovy filets. Stir to blend. Butter a 1 1/2 quart baking dish. Place half the potato slices in it; cover with half the onion/anchovy mixture and repeat. Carefully pour in the milk, sprinkle bread crumbs on top, dot with remaining butter, and bake in a 325° oven for approximately one hour or until potatoes are soft and most of the milk has been absorbed. Serves 4 to 6.

ACETARIES, WORTES, AND OTHER SAVOURY ACCOMPANIMENTS

The Devil's Garden

The onion, so the story goes, was the direct result of Satan's visit to the Garden of Eden. When he stepped out of Paradise after tempting Man to his downfall, his footprints were distinct and pronounced. Where his right foot fell, an onion plant sprang up; in his left footprint garlic grew. Leeks planted themselves where his tail dragged on the ground.

Members of the onion family are some of the oldest vegetables known along with turnips, radishes, and melons. In Roman times, onions were a favorite sweetened delicacy. It is said that two of Cleopatra's favorite foods were candied melon with stuffed onion. Along with a hunk of bread and a piece of cheese, onions were the sustenance of travelers, and for centuries they were the mainstay of poor folk.

We are more fortunate. The wide variety of fresh vegetables for sale in supermarkets or at a farmer's wayside stand gives us more choices than the first kitchen gardeners could ever imagine. With modern transportation, we are even able to choose among exotic plants from Asia and Africa.

While vegetables are good and good for us, their nutrients can be lost by over-cooking. It is important to use a simple method of cooking, steaming for instance, that will result in a tender-crisp, flavorful complement to the meal.

ACETARIA

Acetaria is an old word for vegetables that are eaten raw; in other words, salad ingredients. In 1697 John Evelyn wrote a book titled *Acetaria: A Discourse on Sallets*. I have not seen that little book but the following recipe from it was quoted by both Alice Cooke Brown and Eleanor Sinclair Rhode in their books about herbs. One should remember that herbs are defined as any plants that have a soft fleshy stem as opposed to the woody stalks of shrubs and trees. John Evelyn's instructions seem just as useful now as when they were written over 300 years ago. Note the directions for something like mayonnaise, though I'm not sure what is meant by "cut into quarters."

Recipe for the perfect Sallet

1. Let your Herby ingredients be exquisitely cull'd . . . discreetly sprinkled, then overmuch sob'd with Spring-Water, especially Lettuce . . . let them remain a while in the Cullender to drain the superuous moisture: And lastly, swing them altogether gently in a clean coarse Napkin.

2. The Oyl must be very clean, not high-colour'd nor yellow: but with an Eye rather of pallid, olive green, without Smell, or the least touch of rancid, or indeed of any sensible Taste or Scent at all . . .

3. Vinegar and other liquid Acids, perfectly clear, neither sawre, Vapid or spent . . .

4. The Salt should be detersive, penetrating, quickning and of the brightest Bay grey-Salt.

5. Mustard should be of the best Tewksberry; or else compos'd of the soundest and weightiest Yorkshire Seed.

6. Pepper should be not bruised to too small a dust.

7. Yolks of fresh and new-laid Eggs, boiled moderately hard, to be mingl'd and mash'd with the Mustard, Oyl and Vinegar and part to cut into quarters, and eat with the Herbs.

8. The knife with which the Sallet Herbs are cut be of Silver and by no means of Steel, which all Acids are apt to corrode, and retain a Metalic relish of.

9. The Saldiere ought to be of Porcelane, or of the Holland-Delft Ware.

SWEET SURPRISE

Since sweet peppers now come to market all year long, and in several shades of red, orange, yellow, and green, this salad can be served any time you would like to offer a sweet surprise. It would be perfect for a Christmas meal when made with holiday colors.

2 medium sweet peppers
1 3-ounce package cream cheese, softened
1/3 cup salad oil
1/3 cup ketchup
1 tablespoon chopped fresh parsley
1/2 teaspoon onion salt
1/2 teaspoon sugar
2 tablespoons vinegar
Carrot curls and radish roses
Lettuce

Make ketchup dressing by combining all ingredients except cheese and peppers. Beat or shake well for thorough blending.

Cut off tops of peppers and remove seeds and white membranes. Using a mixer, blend 1 1/2 tablespoons dressing with the softened cream cheese until well mixed and fluffy. Fill peppers with the mixture, and chill for several hours. When ready to serve, cut in thin slices, lay on bed of lettuce, and garnish with radish roses and carrot curls. Pass the dressing.

To make carrot curls: peel a carrot and trim off ends. Using the peeler, shave off thin slices, then coil each slice and fasten with a tooth pick. Place in ice water for several hours. Remove toothpicks before using.

To make the radish roses: wash radishes and cut off ends. Stand radish upright, slice down two-thirds of the way, being careful not to cut the slice off. Make three more cuts around the radish. Place in bowl of ice water for several hours and they will open up.

WORTES

Worte is a Medieval English term for any leafy green vegetable and members of the onion family as well as the seasoning herbs. We use it today as a suffix for some garden plants like *spiderwort* or *milkwort*. Wortes differ from acetaries by being cooked rather than eaten raw. In his eBook, *A Chaucerian Cookery,* James L. Matterer cites this 14th-century receipt for Buttered Wortes:

Take al manor of good herbes that thou may gete, and do bi ham as is forsaid; putte hem on the fire with faire water; put ther-to clarefied buttur a grete quantite. Whan thei ben boyled ynough, salt hem; late none otemele come ther-in. Dise brede small in disshes, and powre on the wortes, and serue hem forth.

And here is a modern adaptation:

1 large head of cabbage, shredded OR
8 cups of mixed greens
2 or 3 leeks, cut into rounds
1/2 cup fresh parsley, loosely chopped
4 tablespoons butter
Salt to taste
1 cup croutons or diced stale bread

Bring a pot of water to a boil. Add cabbage or greens, leeks, parsley, and butter; cook until just tender. Drain vegetables and salt as desired. Place croutons or bread in bottom of a serving dish and pour the greens over. Serves 6.

PUFF BALLS

Originating in the Andean region of Peru and Chile where over 100 varieties are found, potatoes were introduced into Europe in the early 16ᵗʰ century and made their way to our country soon after. They are the fourth largest food crop after rice, wheat, and maize. I believe most of us think of Idaho or Maine when asked where potatoes grow, but what you buy in a supermarket could just as easily have come from China, which is currently the largest potato producer in the world.

Adapted from *The Yankee Cookbook,* here is a potato recipe from Maine.

6 or 7 medium potatoes
3 tablespoons butter
1/2 cup hot milk
1/3 cup grated cheese
Salt and pepper to taste
1 egg, beaten
1/2 cup bread crumbs

Peel and boil potatoes until soft, then mash and stir to make them smooth. Add the butter, hot milk, cheese, salt, and pepper and beat until the mixture is light and fluffy. While still hot, shape into small balls, roll in the beaten egg and then in bread crumbs, and place on a well-greased cookie sheet. Toast to a nice brown in a 450° oven. Serve immediately to 6.

SCOOTIN'-'LONG-THE-SHORE

When New England fishermen returned from a morning of fishing they still had a lot of unloading to do even though they had worked up good appetites. Frequently they clamored for Scootin'-'long-the-Shore, a meal which could be easily prepared over an open fire right there on the beach.
Bacon fat, onions, and potatoes are all that are needed for this dish with a fanciful name. The amounts of each are governed by how many folks are ready to eat.

Sometimes they rendered down salt pork and used that fat for frying, with the chitlings added in when the potatoes were cooked. In Maine, this dish was known as VERY POOR MAN'S DINNER.

Another potato and onion dish is NECESSITY MESS, or TILTON'S GLORY. It comes from Martha's Vineyard. The onions are fried with diced salt pork, preferably in a cast iron Dutch oven. When the onions are good and brown, add peeled, sliced potatoes, cover with water, and cook until potatoes are done. Sometimes carrots or turnip were added, but they really didn't qualify as necessities!

RUTABAGA DOLLARS

Rootabaga Stories, a book of wonderfully fanciful stories written for children by Carl Sandberg many years ago, served to attach a glimmer of immortality to the lowly rutabaga. Known in England as a *swede,* we call it rutabaga from the Swedish word *rotabagge* and know it more familiarly as yellow turnip. While the strong flavor of rutabaga is objectionable to many folks, others find it heartening. It is best combined with other foods – cheese, potato, apples – and seasoned with the complementary flavors of various spices – cinnamon, nutmeg, mace. These rutabaga dollars are particularly good with baked ham.

1 very large rutabaga OR
2 medium ones
2 tablespoons brown sugar
Pinch of salt
1/2 teaspoon nutmeg
1/4 teaspoon cinnamon
1-2 tablespoons butter

Peel the rutabaga, then cut in 1/2-inch slices. Cook in water until tender but still firm. (Test with a fork.)When cool enough to handle and using a round cookie cutter, cut circles approximately 1 1/2 inches in diameter. Arrange the "dollars" in a greased shallow pan. Combine the sugar, salt, and spices and sprinkle over the rutabaga. Dot each circle with butter. Bake at 375° for 20 to 30 minutes. Serves 4 to 6.

Save leftover scraps of rutabaga to mash with potato or apple for another meal.

SUMMER SACCATASH

From her book *New Receipts for Cooking* written in the mid-1800's, this is Miss Leslie's recipe for Summer Saccatash:

"String a quarter of a peck of young green beans, and cut each bean into three pieces (not more) and do not split them. Have by you a pan of cold water and throw the beans into it as you cut them. Have ready over the fire a pot or saucepan of boiling water, put in the beans and boil them hard near twenty minutes. Afterwards take them up and drain them well through a cullender. Take half a dozen ears of young but full-grown Indian corn (or eight or nine if they are not all large) and cut the grains down from the cob. Mix together the corn and the beans, adding a very small teaspoonful of salt, and boil them about twenty minutes. Then take up the saccatash, drain it well through a sieve, put it into a deep dish, and while hot mix in a large piece of butter, (at least the size of an egg,) add some pepper, and send it to the table. It is generally eaten with salted or smoked meat."

Everything was so different in those days! I had always thought of succotash as a combination of corn and lima beans or butter beans (and the word itself spelled with a *u,* not an *a),* but on our farm in New Hampshire in the summer when the Kentucky Wonder string beans were young and tender we used Miss Leslie's recipe whenever we had leftover corn on the cob and were delighted with the different flavor and texture.

No need to write out measurements: just use equal quantities of tender green beans and corn kernels. The beans certainly do not need the long cooking Miss Leslie suggests and I do believe a smaller bit of butter will do quite as well as her egg-sized piece. Don't forget to cut the beans into just three pieces!

RABBITS' CHOICE

There aren't very many oddly named recipes for vegetables. Their preparation and cooking are usually pretty straightforward, so I was pleased to come across this recipe while browsing in a used book store. It was written on a scrap of paper being used as a bookmark.

6 medium carrots
1 6-8" sweet potato
2 tablespoons butter
A pinch each of cinnamon, nutmeg, and mace
Salt and pepper to taste

Peel and cut carrots and sweet potatoes into small pieces. There should be about 2 cups of each vegetable. Cook in separate pots until tender; carrots take longer than sweet potatoes. Drain the liquid (save it for the soup pot), and combine the two. Sprinkle the spices over all, dot with butter, and stir vigorously until well blended. Serves 6.

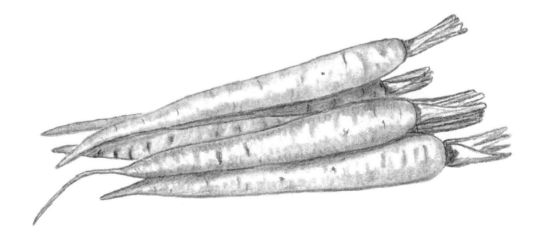

WHITE CLOUD

I have a feeling that the person who named this recipe was a housewife and mother whose family consisted of picky eaters. Cauliflower is one of those cabbage family of vegetables that children don't take to very easily, but by disguising this dish to resemble mashed potatoes no doubt she hoped to entice them into trying it. I've had this recipe in my collection since the 1970s, cut from a page in a magazine, and I tried it on my own family with surprisingly good results. I found it an easy and tasty way of preparing cauliflower, albeit an unusual one.

1 medium cauliflower
1/4 cup ranch dressing
Salt and pepper to taste
Fresh parsley for garnish

Wash and cut the cauliflower into small florets, discarding the tough stems. Cook in water until soft and falling apart. Drain, then return to pot. Add the ranch dressing and stir, mash, and whip until there is a resemblance to mashed potatoes. If needed, season with salt and pepper. Garnish with fresh parsley. Serves 4 to 6, depending on the size of the head of cauliflower.

DREAM BOATS

Every summer, in New London, New Hampshire, the same admonishments were heard from anyone you passed: "Lock the car! Roll up the windows!" "If you haven't locked your car, you will find it filled with zucchini!" The problem, of course, was that everyone's zucchini plants all started producing at once; we were all overwhelmed at the same time. One of the secrets to survival was to pick the squash while it was still very young and tender. The older and larger they got, the more you had to use and use up.

This recipe using tender young zucchini was given to me by my dear friend, Clara Sawyer. She said it was the best way she had found to get her family to enjoy zucchini as a vegetable side dish. (They had no problems with zucchini bread, cake, or cookies!) My family was won over, too, and we decided that Clara was right: Dream Boats was a good name for them.

6 young zucchini – 6-8 inches long
1 3-ounce package cream cheese
2 tablespoons minced onion
1 cup sour cream
Salt and pepper to taste
Paprika

Place whole, unpeeled zucchini in enough boiling water to cover them. Do not cover pot. Reduce heat and simmer about 10 minutes until squash is nearly tender. Remove from pot. When cool enough to handle, slice in half lengthwise and scoop out seeds into a bowl. Mix the seeds with cream cheese, onion, salt and pepper and spoon in equal portions into the "boats." Arrange in a buttered pan. Spoon sour cream evenly over each one; sprinkle with a dash of paprika. Bake about 10 minutes in a 325° oven. Serves 6.

Note: Clara said that some folks like a cheesier flavor so you could add some grated cheddar cheese to the stuffing mix – perhaps 1/4-1/2 cup.

RED FLANNELS

There must be as many different recipes for this Yankee dish as there are cooks in New England. Some call for leftover corned beef; others use ground meat; and still others, as here, are plain enough to be served as a side dish with any entrée. Use a seasoned cast iron frying pan if you have one.

Cooked beets
Cooked potatoes
Chopped raw onion
Bacon or other fat for frying

Chop beets into small pieces. Measure the amount of beets and then chop one-third that amount of potatoes. Sauté the onion in enough bacon fat to cover the bottom of a frying pan. When onion is soft, add the potatoes and beets, mixed together, and heat over medium heat until a crust forms on the underside. This may take five minutes or longer. Use a pan to fit the amount of vegetable you have, which should be about a half-inch deep.

COMBO OF COLOR

It takes a bit of effort to cut up all the vegetables in this recipe, but an attractive and appetizing dish is the result. The cornstarch and broth mixture gives just enough body to the vegetables to keep them from losing their identity. The recipe is adapted from a small booklet put out by the Campbell Soup Company a number of years ago.

1 tablespoon cornstarch
1 1/4 cups vegetable broth
1 1/2 tablespoons olive oil
1 cup each, cut in bite-sized pieces: carrot, celery, red pepper, onion
1/2 teaspoon ginger
1/4 teaspoon garlic powder
1 cup broccoli florets, raw
1 cup snow peas, raw

In a bowl, pour the vegetable broth slowly over the cornstarch while stirring and continue to stir until cornstarch is well blended in. Set aside. In a skillet or wok, using medium heat, stir-fry the carrots, celery, peppers, and onions. Stir in the ginger and garlic powder. When vegetables are tender but still crisp add the broccoli and snow peas. Pour the cornstarch mixture over all and continue to cook and stir until mixture boils and thickens. Reduce heat, cover, and cook a few minutes more as necessary until snow peas and broccoli are cooked to your liking. Makes 6 or more large servings.

HOPPIN' JOHN

Hoppin' John should be the first food you eat on New Year's Day: so say folks from our southern states who believe in the good fortune and possible wealth that this mixture of black-eyed peas and rice might bring to them. Add some collard greens, they say, and you will increase your luck. Originally it was survival food for African slaves during the long ocean voyages; in the Caribbean islands it took on Creole overtones; and by the end of the 18th century it had found its way to southern plantation tables.

There are several widely differing stories of how this came to be called Hoppin' John. The one I like best tells of a crippled black man who hawked portions of it hopping through the streets of Charleston, South Carolina. And there are many variations on the recipe. This is one of the simplest.

1 cup dried black-eyed peas
5 to 6 cups water
Crushed red pepper, to taste
1 smoked ham hock
1 medium onion, chopped
1 cup long-grain white rice

Rinse and pick over the peas to eliminate any pebbles or dirt. Place in large saucepan; add the water, crushed pepper, ham hock, and chopped onion. Simmer uncovered for 1 to 1 1/2 hours or until peas are tender and there are about two cups of liquid remaining. Remove ham hock. Add rice to pot, cover, and continue simmering until rice is cooked and water is absorbed. Meanwhile, cut meat from ham hock and add to pot just before serving. Serves 6 to 8.

THE STAFF OF LIFE: VARIATIONS ON AN OLD THEME

"Bread is a generous gift of nature, a food that can be replaced by no other . . . suitable to every time of day, every age of life, and every temperament." (Antoine-Auguste Parmentier).

From the beginning of man's recorded history to the present day, bread, whether made from wheat, corn, rice, or other grains, has been the staff of life.

The first leavened bread was undoubtedly an accidental discovery. The Egyptians had been using a fermenting process to make a type of beer from water-soaked grain. Warmed by the sun, it was a short step to a bubbling sour mixture. When they added it to the dough they were using for flat bread, they created a raised loaf that was much more appealing.

Early Greeks are credited with developing the baking of bread into a professional art form. Using a three-sided, front-loading clay oven, bakers created a wide variety of breads for sale to local homemakers. They are known to have made breads in all sizes and shapes, as well as sweet rolls and cakes. The Romans considered quality: the fine, white loaves were reserved for Senators and other important personages while the coarse, heavy, dark bread was fed to slaves.

It wasn't until the 18th century that anyone thought of enclosing the cooking fire in a clay or metal container or of building an oven into the side of a chimney. It took another century for the stove with oven to be developed. Through the years there have been many marvelous improvements, but I can testify that the old wood-burning cast iron stove of the early 1900s will still do an excellent job with whatever is being cooked or baked.

A few words about handling the yeast and kneading. Is the water too warm or too cool? Will the dough really rise up out of the bowl? And the problem of kneading in all that flour – should I really dump it out on the counter and work it in by hand? What is kneading? Have no fear. Use lukewarm water, the dough will rise, and yes, dump it all out on a floured board or counter when it gets too hard to mix with a spoon. Then the fun begins: it is time to knead the dough.

KNEADING

Kneading is the most important part of making bread. It is the process of working the dough to blend the yeast with the other ingredients, to break down the gluten, and to add air. On a floured board and with floured hands, roll the dough into a ball. Push away from you with the palms of your hands, then pull up what you just pushed away, give the dough a quarter turn and repeat, and repeat, and repeat, for eight to ten minutes until the dough is no longer sticky and has a satiny sheen.

Kneading dough is a wonderful exercise for body and mind. While you are folding, turning, and pushing, you can work out any frustrations whether they are mental or physical. After a few practices, kneading becomes automatic, one's brain is relaxed, problems are solved, and hands, arms, and back have had a workout. In fact, I would say that baking one's own bread is pleasantly beneficial to one's health.

FEATHERBEDS

In New Hampshire, when the snow was on the ground and the wood-burning stove was generous with its warmth, I would be inspired to make a loaf or two of bread or a pan of rolls. There is something very satisfying about bread making. Mothers and grandmothers of yesteryear relied on bread in one form or another to fill out a meal just as we do today. These light and airy rolls are as well suited to summer salad suppers as they are to a wintery stew where they will be good sopping bread. The recipe is adapted from *The Yankee Cookbook.*

1 large potato
1 teaspoon salt
1/3 cup sugar
1/4 cup butter
3/4 cup potato water
1 egg
1 package dry yeast
3 1/4 to 3 3/4 cups flour

Peel the potato, cut in slices or chunks, and boil in salted water to cover. Cook until soft. Drain, saving the water. Combine 3/4 cup hot potato water with sugar and butter, then cool to lukewarm, approximately 110°. Stir in the yeast; let stand 5 to 10 minutes. Beat in the egg and mashed potato; add 3 3/4 cups flour. Add additional flour as needed to make a dough stiff enough to handle. Knead on floured surface until you have a smooth, pliable dough. Place in greased bowl, cover with a towel, and let rise in a warm place until doubled in size. Punch down. With lightly floured hands, pull off small pieces of dough and shape into rolls. Place close together in a greased pan, and let rise until more than doubled in size. Bake in a hot oven, 400°, for 18 to 20 minutes. Makes 12 or more rolls depending on their size.

IS IT JOURNEY, SHAWNEE, OR JONNY CAKE?

There is ample disagreement about the name Johnny Cake. Some say it is a corruption of Journey Cake, a hard cornmeal biscuit that was easily carried in a pocket and was, for a long time, a staple item for travelers. Others believe it was once called Shawnee Cake after the Indians who taught the pilgrims so much about corn and corn meal. Perhaps it was always Johnny Cake and Jonny is just a misspelling. There is disagreement, too, about the color of the meal: New Englanders, especially those from Rhode Island, use yellow corn meal while Southerners seem to prefer white corn meal.

I believe there are just as many variations of the recipe for Johnny Cake as there are ideas about the name. What was once a very simple flat bread or cake is today light and fluffy, or soft and moist, or frequently sweetened with sugar. Where there were once three simple ingredients there are now six to eight. The two recipes below illustrate some of the gradual changes. For a modern recipe for Yankee Corn Bread or Southern Spoon Bread, I refer you to your own favorite cookbook.

Adapted from *The Presidents' Cookbook*, Johnny Cake as prepared by Abigail and served to John Adams and guests:

Combine 1 teaspoon salt with 1/2 cup cornmeal. Pour in 1 cup scalded milk or boiling water gradually. Spread this mixture into a shallow, buttered rectangular pan about 1/4 inch deep. Bake at 350° until crisp. Cut in squares, split, and spread with butter. Serve hot with maple syrup or maple sugar. Serves 4.

My friend, Irma Benton, shared this handwritten recipe from her Grandmother's Receipt Book dated 1888:

1 cup Indian [*sic*:] (this is cornmeal)
1 cup wheat flour
1 cup white flour
3/8 cup molasses
1 3/4 cups buttermilk
1 teaspoon baking soda

There are no directions for mixing; instead there is this note: "or use only milk enough to make soft as you can handle – bake as you would sugar cake." I believe that means use only as much milk as needed to get the consistency of cake batter. Use a well-greased 9 x 13-inch pan and bake at 350° for 25 to 30 minutes.

SALLY LUNN

In the first half of the 18th century, the city of Bath, England, enjoyed a reputation as the most fashionable watering place in all England. Its healing mineral waters had been known since Roman times, but it took Richard "Beau" Nash, a gambler, a dandy, and the undisputed autocrat of Bath society to promote the luxury and comfort that awaited the visitor. Along with the surge in building that resulted in some very fine Georgian homes still standing in Bath came many little shops offering all manner of items, including food.

Often, though, the freshly baked breads and buns were hawked by young street criers. One young girl, Sally Lunn, moved with such grace and dignity while still carefully balancing on her head a basket of the delicate buns and breads baked by her own hands that her name has forever been attached to the recipe for them. Directions for making Sally Lunn vary from one cookbook to another. This recipe is adapted from *The American Heritage Cookbook.*

1 cup milk
1 package dry yeast
1/4 cup butter
1/3 cup sugar
2 eggs
1/2 teaspoon salt
4 to 4 1/2 cups flour
1/3 cup currants or raisins

Scald the milk, cool to lukewarm, then sprinkle the yeast over it. Stir gently to moisten all the yeast and let stand for five minutes. Combine softened butter, sugar, eggs, and salt and mix well. Add yeast and milk mixture. Stir in flour and currants or raisins. The dough will be sticky, more so than regular bread dough, and impossible to knead. Set aside to rise, covered with a towel, until doubled in bulk.

Punch dough down with a spoon and then spoon into greased tube or *kugelhupf* pan, or for buns, into greased muffin pans. Pans should be no more than half full of dough. Cover and let rise again. Bake at 375° for 30 to 40 minutes for bread, or 20 minutes for buns. Serve hot with plenty of butter and jam. Makes 1 large loaf or about 18 buns.

RUSKS

Old-fashioned Rusks were made with yeast. They were more like a sweetened biscuit than the hard, dry toast I remember buying for my babies to cut their teeth on: those would keep a one-year-old happily busy for a long time! Once readily for sale on grocery shelves, they have now been replaced by *biscotti*. This recipe, adapted from *The Yankee Cookbook,* is for a flavorful toast that closely resembles the Italian version. For teething infants, it would be best to omit the spices.

2 cups plus 2 tablespoons flour
1 teaspoon soda
1/4 teaspoon salt
1 teaspoon nutmeg
1 teaspoon cinnamon
1/2 teaspoon cloves
3/4 cup sugar
1/2 cup shortening
1 egg, beaten
1 cup sour milk

Mix and sift dry ingredients together; cream shortening and sugar. Add egg to butter mixture, then add milk and dry ingredients alternately. Mix well. Spread into a greased 9 x 13-inch pan and bake at 350° for one hour. Cool on racks. Cut into thin slices about 4 inches long and spread out on a second cookie sheet. Return rusks to oven and bake for several hours at 200° or until bread is completely dry and hard. Stored in an airtight container, these will keep for several months. Makes about 30.

ANADAMA

Once upon a time there was a farmer, or perhaps he was a fisherman, or he might have been a logger (it depends on who is telling the story). This man's wife, Anna, was good about having his dinner ready when he got home from a hard day's work. However, it was always the same thing every night: corn-meal mixed with molasses, again and again. One night the man decided he'd had enough. He grabbed his bowl of cornmeal and molasses gruel and stormed over to the pantry and started adding flour, salt, sugar, water, and mixed it all together. Then he put it in a pan and threw it in the oven. When his "bread" was done he resumed his seat at the table and ate it with pleasure, all the time muttering, "Anna, damn, her!" And that is how this early American bread, typical of New England, got its name - or so they say.

1/2 cup yellow corn meal
3/4 cup boiling water
1/4 cup molasses
3 tablespoons butter
1 package dry yeast
1/4 cup warm water
1 tablespoon sugar
1 teaspoon salt
3 cups flour

Combine boiling water, molasses, butter, sugar, and salt in large bowl. Let stand until lukewarm. Soften yeast in 1/4 cup warm water, then stir yeast and half the flour into molasses and cornmeal mixture. Beat well. Stir in remaining flour to form soft ball of dough. Turn out on floured board and knead until smooth and no longer sticky. Place in greased loaf pan which has been lightly sprinkled with additional corn meal, cover with a cloth and allow to rise until doubled in bulk. Punch down, shape into a loaf and bake in a greased 9 x 5-inch pan at 350° for 50 minutes. Makes 1 loaf.

GOLDEN GLOW

This recipe for a "specialty" bread is adapted from *Woman's Day Encyclopedia of Cookery.* My family enjoyed the change in flavor and texture from more ordinary breads.

1 package dry yeast
1/4 cup lukewarm water
2 tablespoons sugar
1 teaspoon salt
1 1/2 cups milk
3 tablespoons salad oil
2 cups grated cheddar cheese
1/2 cup grated raw carrot
5 to 5 1/2 cups flour

Sprinkle yeast on lukewarm water, stir gently to moisten, and let stand for five minutes. Stir in all ingredients except flour, mixing well to dissolve the sugar. Add about half the flour; beat until well blended. Add enough more flour to make a stiff dough that leaves the side of the bowl. Turn out on floured board and knead until the dough becomes smooth and satiny. Place dough in greased bowl, turning over once to grease the top, cover with a towel, and let rise until doubled in bulk. Punch down. Divide dough in half; shape each half to fit a 9 x 5 x 3-inch greased loaf pan. Bake in a 350° oven for 40 minutes. Remove bread from pan and allow to cool on a rack. Makes two loaves.

TOM PIPERSON'S PIG
AND OTHER FAIRINGS

Fairing is an English term for a souvenir given or purchased at a fair. It could be anything that might be on display or for sale. Here I am limiting the word to mean *cookie,* which is an American word taken from the Dutch *koekje,* for small cake. Whatever we call them, they are possibly the most popular food of all, especially with children. Who doesn't like a chocolate chip cookie or a gingersnap or any other variety? What child doesn't come a-running when he or she smells that sweet aroma as a pan of cookies comes out of the oven or, even better, when Mom says, "Let's make some cookies"?

Several of the recipes given here use molasses as their sweetening agent. For a while I thought this was specific in recipes from New England, but it isn't. Molasses was just as important for the early settlers as any other commodity they might need and it went with them as they forged their way west. Until the development of modern refining equipment in the 20th century, molasses was cheaper and more readily available than sugar and according to Miss Leslie, "West India molasses is far more wholesome and nutritious than any other."

Molasses is the byproduct of the sugar-refining process. Sugar cane is crushed, boiled, reboiled, and boiled again to extract as many sugar crystals as possible. The various grades of molasses are the results of the boilings. Blackstrap molasses is the darkest, the most nutritious, and the result of the third boiling. What we buy in the grocery store is usually from the second boiling and is well suited for use in cooking and baking.

There are more recipes for cookies with odd names than for any other food we cook. The recipes here are just a random sampling. I'm sure everyone has their own particular favorite.

TOM PIPERSON'S PIG

Tom, Tom the Piper's son
Stole a pig and away he run

The pig that Tom stole was not a squealing piglet, but a gingerbread *fairing* shaped in the form of a pig. He could just as easily have stolen a rabbit- or chicken-shaped cookie. Anyone who has ever had a good whiff of hot gingerbread will find it not too difficult to imagine medieval Tom and other youngsters like him being tempted to steal and run.

Through the years, recipes for gingerbread have been altered and improved until there are many variations from which to choose. This recipe makes a firm gingerbread dough that is easy to roll out and cut.

4 cups flour
1 teaspoon cinnamon
1 teaspoon ginger
1 teaspoon baking powder
1/2 teaspoon mace
1/2 teaspoon ground cloves
1/2 teaspoon salt
1/2 cup soft butter or margarine
1 cup sugar
3/4 cup molasses
1 egg

Reserving 1/2 cup flour until later, sift together all dry ingredients. Cream butter or margarine with sugar; beat in molasses and egg until well blended. Add dry ingredients in several portions, beating well each time. Add only enough of the remaining 1/2 cup flour to make a medium-stiff dough. Chill dough at least 30 minutes. On a lightly floured surface roll out dough, a fourth at a time, to 1/4-inch thickness. Cut with cookie cutter, place on greased baking sheet, and bake at 350° for 8 to 10 minutes. Do not overbake: molasses will burn very easily – cookies should be done but not browned.

Fairings were often decorated with gold leaf. If you want truly authentic cookies, edible gold leaf is available through the Internet or specialty shops. It is expensive, but a little goes a long way.

JOE FROGGERS

This New England recipe makes good use of the rum and molasses that were traded for wood and other products in the West Indies. The large size was made to satisfy a hungry sailor's desire. There was no indication of where the name originated; perhaps Joe was the mess cook and his cookies resembled frogs.

3 1/2 cups flour
1/2 teaspoon salt
2 teaspoons ginger
1/2 teaspoon cloves
1/2 teaspoon nutmeg
1/4 teaspoon allspice
3/8 cup water
1/8 cup rum
1 teaspoon baking soda
1 cup dark molasses
1/2 cup shortening
1 cups sugar

Sift together flour, spices, and salt. Combine water and rum. Add baking soda to molasses. Cream shortening and sugar; add half the flour, half the water/rum mix, and half the molasses. Blend well after each addition, then repeat with remaining ingredients. Chill dough for several hours or overnight. Roll out on lightly floured surface to 1/4-inch thick. Cut with a 3 or 4-inch round cookie cutter. Bake on a greased cookie sheet at 375° for 10 to 12 minutes until lightly browned. Watch them carefully so they do not burn. Remove from oven; let stand a few minutes before removing from cookie sheet. Makes 2 dozen.

2″

BE
KIND
TO
ALL

4″

1.5″

1″

Hornbook Diagram

HORNBOOKS

In colonial America where sweets were infrequent treats, gingerbread boys were used as rewards for good work. At Christmastime, a child might expect to receive a new hornbook, either real or made of gingerbread. Real hornbooks were in the shape of a paddle, usually made from wood but some times from ivory, bone, lead, or leather. They were the earliest type of school primer. The alphabet (with U and J omitted), numbers, Bible verses, and various proverbs or moral sayings were written on the pages attached to them. A covering of thin, transparent horn was added to protect those pages from grubby little hands - hence the name *hornbook*.

Hornbooks were so much a part of the early American child's life that the "gingerbread horn for Christmas morn to greet the day when Christ was born" seemed a most logical means of ensuring a child's learning abilities. Copying the shape of a hornbook in gingerbread, with letters or short verses spelled out in icing, these were an edible treat for a child that also had special meaning for his parents: for it was believed that "knowledge is thereby devoured by ye childe and a glad yeare with great wealth of learning comes in store." Oh, that it could be so easy!

Cut out a cardboard pattern 4x2 inches with a 1x11/2 inches handle centered in a 2 inches end.

Using the gingerbread recipe for Tom Piperson's Pig, roll the dough as thinly as possible. Cut out hornbooks using your cardboard pattern. Bake as directed. When cool, use decorator icing to write short sayings or a child's name on each hornbook. Makes 8 hornbooks.

For the icing, combine 1 cup confectioner's sugar with 1 tablespoon slightly beaten egg white and beat thoroughly. Use a round toothpick to write with, or you can put the icing in a plastic bag, make a very small cut at one corner, and squeeze gently as you write. This icing dries out quickly; keep any extra covered with a damp cloth.

For several years, I made a batch of these hornbooks with sayings like "Jesus loves you," "Honor your parents," "Be truthful," and donated them for sale at our church bazaar at Christmastime. They sold quickly!

SCOTCH TEAS

These Scotch Teas are crisp, lusciously sweet, and full of wholesome fiber. They are well-named as they would be right at home on the tea tray beside dainty cucumber sandwiches.

1 egg
1/2 cup sugar
2 teaspoons melted butter
1 cup quick-cooking oats (uncooked)
1/8 teaspoon salt
1/2 teaspoon vanilla

Preheat oven to 350° and move oven rack to highest level. Grease a cookie sheet (preferably non-stick) very, very well.

Beat the egg in a large bowl. Continue beating as you add the sugar gradually; stir in remaining ingredients. Take up rounded teaspoonfuls of the mixture and push on to pan about inch apart. (I used two teaspoons to do this.) Flatten and shape each little mound with back of spoon. Bake on top shelf of oven until delicately browned or about 10 minutes. While still hot, remove to wire rack to cool. Makes about 20 delicate cookies.

LUMBERJACKS

This recipe was given to me by my daughter-in-law who said she had gotten it directly from a "mountain man" when she was hiking in the Rockies. I'm not sure I believe her story entirely, but no matter, these are spicy and delicious.

1 cup sugar
1 cup butter
1 cup dark molasses
2 cggs
4 cups flour
1 teaspoon soda
1/4 teaspoon salt
2 teaspoons cinnamon
1 teaspoon ginger

Cream sugar and shortening; add molasses and eggs. Beat well, then add sifted dry ingredients and mix well. Roll into small balls and place on greased cookie sheet. Flatten each ball with the bottom of a glass which has been greased and then dipped in granulated sugar. Bake at 350° for 12 to 15 minutes.

ROCKS

The popularity of these cookies appears to be widespread. I have found recipes for them in cookbooks from New England, Minnesota, and Idaho. In *Mrs. Curtis's Cook Book,* published in 1908, they are called Oklahoma Rocks. James Beard has written about Rocks that "surely I ate nearly a ton of these when I was a child." These cookies are so easy to make, and they improve with age if stored in an airtight container.

Of the many recipes there are, this is the one I like best:

1/2 cup soft butter
1 cup brown sugar, packed
2 eggs
1/3 cup boiling water
2 cups seeded raisins
1/2 cup chopped walnuts
2 1/2 cups sifted flour
1 teaspoon baking powder
1/4 teaspoon salt
1 1/2 teaspoons cinnamon

Pour boiling water over the raisins in a shallow dish. Allow to cool. (This step may be omitted but it does help to plump up the raisins.)

Cream butter, add sugar and slightly beaten eggs. Beat until light and well blended. Sift dry ingredients together; add to butter/egg mixture along with the walnuts. Add soaked raisins and water and mix well. Drop by teaspoonfuls onto greased cookie sheet; bake in 350° oven about 15 minutes. Makes 3 dozen knobby and tasty, cookies.

HAYSTACKS

Dark chocolate, nuts, and unsweetened cereal – what else could be combined so easily for a healthy snack? And the recipe is simple enough for a child to follow!

1 6-ounce package chocolate chips
1/2 cup chopped nuts
2 1/2 cups ready-to-eat cereal – wheat or corn flakes, rice or wheat puffs

Melt chocolate chips in the top of a double boiler over boiling water. Add nuts and cereal and mix well. Remove from heat. Drop by tablespoon onto waxed paper; refrigerate. Makes about 2 dozen haystacks.

PINE TREE SHILLINGS

I wish I could be sure that this is a recipe from Maine, but I am not. The pine is Maine's state tree, shillings are old English money; this could very well be an old family recipe. I found it printed on a piece of paper tucked into a book in a used book store in Virginia.

1 cup light molasses
1/2 cup brown sugar
1/2 cup butter
3 cups flour
1/2 teaspoon baking soda
Pinch of salt
1 teaspoon cinnamon
1/2 teaspoon ginger

In a saucepan heat the molasses, add the butter, and stir until the butter is melted and the two are well blended. Stir in the brown sugar and let the mixture cool. Sift together the dry ingredients and add to the cooled molasses mixture. Beat well. Shape dough into two rolls about one inch in diameter and chill in the refrigerator for eight hours or overnight.

When ready to bake, slice very thin, and place on a greased cookie sheet about three inches apart. Keep the dough in the refrigerator except when you are actually slicing it. Bake at 375° about 10 minutes. This dough will keep for several weeks in the refrigerator. Makes 4 dozen.

QUAKERS

Oats, the principal ingredient in this recipe, have been around for many millennia, but it was not until well into the Middle Ages that they were acknowledged to be nourishing food for humans as well as animals. Oats grow abundantly in Scotland and from there were brought to America. It took an enterprising immigrant from Germany to develop a method of steel-cutting and rolling the groats (hulled grain) to produce a finer and more palatable meal. In 1877, Henry D. Seymour chose the man in Quaker garb to be his now very familiar trademark.

This recipe for plain oatmeal cookies was with the one for Pine Tree Shillings. I've left it as it was printed, but I prefer to reduce the amount of sugar to 1 1/3 cups.

2 cups brown sugar
1 cup butter
2 eggs, beaten
2 cups flour
1 1/2 teaspoons baking soda
Pinch of salt
3 cups quick Quaker Oats
2 teaspoons vanilla
White sugar

Cream together sugar and butter until well blended. Add beaten eggs and vanilla. Sift flour with soda and salt, stir in the oats, and add to the batter. Pour a small amount of white sugar in a bowl; dip your fingers in the sugar to keep dough from sticking to them as you shape it into balls about the size of a walnut. Roll each ball in the sugar, then place on a greased cookie sheet about 3 inches apart. Bake at 375° for 12 to 15 minutes. Makes 4 dozen large, soft cookies.

Recommended by Peg

WHIFFENPOUFFERS

I found this recipe tucked among the pages of a small, privately printed book of poetry that I picked up at a garage sale. An identical recipe cut from a newspaper is titled BULLETS or you can give bits of the dough a crescent moon shape and you will have CRESCENTS.

These are easy to make, very nutty, and not at all sweet. They would be good served with a light dessert.

1/2 cup butter
2 tablespoons sugar
1 cup chopped nuts
1 teaspoon vanilla
1 cup flour
1/8 teaspoon salt

Cream butter and sugar; add vanilla, salt, and nuts. Blend, then stir in flour and mix well. Form balls about the size of a small walnut, place on greased cookie sheet, and bake at 350° for 20 minutes. Makes 2 dozen.

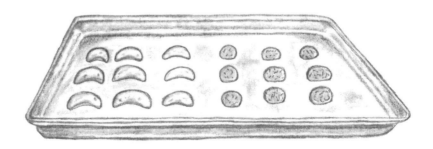

HERMITS

These chewy, rich cookie bars have been a family favorite for years, ever since I first obtained the recipe from my husband's brother who made them regularly for his children. It is said to have originated in New England when those adventurous sea-faring men brought back exotic fruits and spices from the Indies.

1/2 cup butter
1/2 cup sugar
2 eggs
1/2 cup molasses
2 cups flour
1/4 teaspoon salt
3/4 teaspoon cream of tartar
1 teaspoon cinnamon
1/2 teaspoon cloves
1/4 teaspoon each mace, nutmeg, allspice
1/2 cup chopped raisins
1/2 cup currants
1/2 cup chopped walnuts

Cream butter and sugar until light and fluffy; add well-beaten eggs and molasses. Beat well. Sift together flour, salt, and spices. Use 1/4 cup for coating raisins, currants, and nuts to keep them from sticking together, then combine everything, mix well, and spread evenly – about 1/2 inch thick – on a well-greased rectangular cookie pan. Bake at 350° about 18 minutes or until toothpick inserted in center comes out clean. Cut in bars while still warm.
Makes about 4 dozen.

SNICKERDOODLES

Quick and easy, these snickerdoodles never fail to please. They were definitely my children's favorites. I learned very early that the size of the cookie did not matter as much as the number of cookies given. There seemed to be an unwritten rule that there should be a cookie for each hand. If they were large cookies, so much the better, but two small ones would be better than just one large. It took several years for the children to outgrow that notion and to realize that bigger is better when it concerns sugar cookies.

1 cup shortening
1 1/2 cups sugar
2 eggs
2 3/4 cups flour
2 teaspoons cream of tartar
1 teaspoon baking soda
2 tablespoons sugar
2 teaspoons cinnamon

Cream butter and sugar together, then beat in the eggs. Sift dry ingredients together except the 2 tablespoons of sugar and the cinnamon. Add dry ingredients to creamed mixture and mix well. Chill dough for several hours. Roll bits of dough into small balls; coat each with the sugar and cinnamon which have been mixed together. Place coated balls on an ungreased baking sheet about 2 inches apart. Bake at 400° for 8 to 10 minutes. Makes 4 to 5 dozen.

PALM LEAVES AND PIG'S EARS

These are not strictly cookies since they are made with pie dough instead of the usual cakelike mixture. They take time to make, but they are a delightful change from the usual round cookie. Try them for a special treat.

1 package prepared pie crust or use your own favorite recipe
Honey
Finely chopped nuts

On surface dusted with granulated sugar (instead of flour), roll out pie crust into a rectangle 1/4-inch thick. Lightly draw a centerline lengthwise and then with each long side make three folds toward center (see below). Slice about a 1/2-inch wide. Place 2 inches apart on a greased baking sheet. Let the Palm Leaves rest about 30 minutes, and then bake at 400° for 10 to 12 minutes. The bottoms should be a nice golden brown. Turn them over and return to oven for a few minutes more. Brush with honey while still warm and sprinkle with chopped nuts if desired.

FLUMMERIES, FOOLS, AND SWEETS OF SUCH ILK

By the time the Tudors came to the British throne in the late 15th century, many new foods were being brought into England from foreign lands. People began to experiment with different food combinations. Oranges and lemons were new flavorful treats, sugar was more readily available though still very expensive, and flowers, especially roses, were used as colorful decoration as well as for the perfume they exuded. It was at this time that fruit and custard dishes were developed and were served with the meats, fish, and vegetables. Dessert as a finishing touch to a meal did not come until later.

Whether you choose to serve a flummery or a grunt, a pie or a cake covered in icing, or just a sliced apple, dessert determines how we feel when we leave the table. Meat and potatoes are taken for granted, but desserts are just for fun. To add to the fun, unknown folks have given us recipes with such fanciful names as fool, buckle, sponge, and many others. Plan your dessert to fit your meal, and everyone will leave the table in a happy mood.

FLUMMERIES, FOOLS, AND SPONGES

These are summer desserts. They are fruity, light, refreshing, and easy to prepare. They differ only in the ingredient that is used to bind the fruit together: whipped cream, egg whites, cornstarch, or gelatin. Almost any fruit can be used. I recently made a delicious Sponge using rhubarb, strawberries and orange flavored gelatin.

Flummery

3 cups berries or crushed fruit
2 cups water
3/4 cup sugar
4 tablespoons cornstarch
1/4 cup cold water

Simmer berries or fresh fruit in two cups water until just softened. Dissolve cornstarch in the cold water and stir into fruit. Add sugar and cook, stirring constantly, until thick and smooth, about 8 to 10 minutes. Pour into 6 serving dishes. Serve very cold topped with whipped cream if desired.

Fool

2 cups berries
Sugar to taste
1 cup cream, whipped OR
3 egg whites, stiffly beaten OR
1 16-ounce carton whipped topping

Prepare fruit an hour or so before serving. Mash berries slightly with a fork to allow juices to run. Sweeten to taste and let stand, covered, until dessert time. Just before serving, whip cream, egg whites or topping until stiff. Fold in berries so that they are well mixed in, but use a light touch. A fool should be light and fluffy – billowy. Spoon into dessert dishes and garnish with whole berries or mint leaves. Makes 6 portions.

Sponge

2 cups crushed fruit
1 cup water or juice
1 3-ounce package fruit-flavored gelatin
1 cup whipped cream

Heat fruit and water together till boiling; add gelatin and stir until it is completely dissolved. Chill until mixture begins to firm up. Fold in whipped cream; chill for several more hours before serving. Serves 4 to 6.

FLOATING ISLAND

This old-fashioned custard dessert, also known as SNOW EGGS, is rarely heard of nowadays. The recipe brings back memories of my youth. My grandmother served it to me often because, she said, it was so <u>good</u> for me. It is an easy, but nourishing, finale to any meal.

3 egg yolks
1 teaspoon flour
1/4 cup sugar
2 1/2 cups milk
1 teaspoon vanilla
Pinch of salt

For the meringue:

3 egg whites
4 tablespoons sugar
1/2 teaspoon almond extract

Beat the egg yolks with a whisk in the upper part of a double boiler over boiling water. Mix together flour, sugar, and salt, and stir into egg. Add the milk and cook over simmering water, stirring several times until the mixture will coat and cling to a silver spoon. This will take approximately 15 to 20 minutes. Remove pan from heat, add the vanilla, and stir one more time.

Beat the egg whites until stiff. Gradually add the sugar as you continue beating and then the almond extract. Place meringue in a serving dish and pour the custard over it. Use a few folding strokes with a rubber scraper to float some of the meringue (the island) to the top. Chill thoroughly. Serves 4.

If you prefer, the meringue may be baked before floating it in the custard. Drop by spoonful into a shallow pan of hot water, and then set the pan in a 350° oven for 20 minutes. Remove meringues using a slotted spoon and slip on top of the custard in a serving dish.

TRIFLE

In New Hampshire, when fresh peaches were available and the black raspberry bushes were still producing luscious berries, I served Trifle to the Happy Hookers, our Ladies Rug Hooking Group. They were duly impressed with the presentation and delighted with the blending of tastes and textures. There is nothing trifling about this dessert: it can be elegant when served in a delicate glass trifle bowl. Since I don't own one, I used a white ironstone bowl about four inches deep and nine inches in diameter and it still made quite an impression.

TRIFLE was brought to us by early English settlers. Perhaps in an attempt to disavow their origins or because of the inclusion of sherry they also called it TIPSY PARSON or TIPSY SQUIRE. There are many variations in the recipes for Trifle – it can be as simple or as elaborate as your imagination dictates. This is what I served the Ladies.

Plain yellow cake
2 large ripe peaches
2 cups black raspberries
1/8 cup sherry or fruit juice
1 package instant vanilla pudding mix
1 cup heavy cream, whipped OR
2 cups whipped topping

Mix pudding according to directions and set aside to thicken. Cut the cake into slices about a 1/2-inch thick, and line the bottom and sides of the bowl with them. Drizzle sherry or fruit juice over the cake. Peel and slice peaches and put them on the cake with half the black raspberries. Spoon pudding on top of peaches and top it with whipped cream spread evenly over all. Garnish with a circle of the remaining black raspberries. Makes 10 to 12 servings.

BLACK BUCKLE

Buckles, Cobblers, Grunts, Sizzlers, and Slumps are all desserts that combine fruit with dough of some kind. Grunt is the Cape Cod term for a steamed berry pudding; a Sizzler is similar to a fried pie; and Slumps are topped with dumplings that are steamed in the cooked fruit. Cobblers are a cross between a pie and a pudding, while Buckles are somewhere between cake and pudding. All of these desserts have their origins in the early days of colonization when housewives were imaginative in the ways that they used whatever they could find that was edible. While this recipe specifically calls for black plums, almost any fruit or berry can be used.

4 cups sliced fresh black plums
1/3 cup soft butter
1/2 cup sugar
1 teaspoon vanilla
1 egg
1 1/2 cups flour
1 1/2 teaspoons baking powder
1/8 teaspoon salt
1/2 cup milk

Cream butter and sugar; add egg and vanilla. Sift together dry ingredients and add alternately with the milk. Lightly grease an attractive baking dish (about the size of a 9x9-inch pan). Spread batter evenly in dish. Arrange the plums on top. Cover with topping.

Topping:

1/4 cup flour
1/2 cup sugar
1/4 cup butter
1 teaspoon cinnamon

Work ingredients together with fingers until mixture is like coarse meal. Spread evenly over plums. Bake at 350° for 35 to 40 minutes. Makes about 8 servings.

BROWN BETTY

This is another of those old recipes that were standbys as I was growing up. For those of us who have never quite mastered the art of making a crisp pie crust, this recipe will please your family almost as much as a slice of apple pie. It lacks all the fat of a pie crust while retaining the flavor and texture of an apple pie.

2 cups cubed, day-old bread
4 cups peeled, sliced apples
1/2 cup brown sugar
1/4 cup hot water
1/2 teaspoon cinnamon
1/4 teaspoon nutmeg or mace
1 1/2 tablespoons lemon juice
Grated rind of 1/2 lemon
2 tablespoons melted butter

Place one-third of the cubed bread in the bottom of a buttered baking dish. Top with half the apples and half of all other ingredients except melted butter. Add another third of the crumbs. Place remaining apples and flavorings on top. Mix remaining crumbs with melted butter and spread on top of apples. Cover the dish and bake in a 375° oven for half an hour. Remove cover and continue baking until apples are cooked and crumbs are brown, another 15 minutes or so. Serve with whipped cream or ice cream. Serves 4 to 6.

DUTCH BABIES

This is another of those eye-catching finds torn from the page of a magazine. Unfortunately I did not note which magazine or its date; however I have served this dessert to guests on several occasions and it was always well received. You will recognize the batter ingredients and method of preparation as a variant of Popovers. I prefer to use fresh berries, cut up if necessary, whenever they are available, but pie filling works well, too.

6 eggs
3/4 cup flour
Pinch of salt
1 cup milk
Cherry pie filling (or other flavor) or sliced strawberries or other berries
Whipped cream
Garnish

Beat eggs until foamy; add flour and salt alternately with milk. Beat well after each addition. Heat six 10-ounce custard cups in 425° oven until hot. Pour about 1/2 cup of batter in each hot cup. Bake at 425° for 20 minutes. Prick centers with fork several times, reduce heat to 350°, and bake for ten minutes longer.

Fill centers with pie filling or fresh berries which have been lightly sweetened. Top with whipped cream and a cherry or berry for garnish. Serve warm to six delighted folks.

Note: this recipe may also be used for making CREAM PUFFS, if you would prefer a custard filling in place of the fruit.

SPICED INDIAN

This recipe for Indian pudding made with corn meal and molasses is one of the earliest to be handed down through the generations. It is strictly an American dessert. The pilgrims, needing all the help they could get from the native Indians, must have been very grateful when they were first introduced to corn and corn meal. The recipe is adapted from *The New England Yankee Cookbook.*

5 cups milk
3/4 cup dark molasses
1/4 cup sugar
1/2 cup yellow cornmeal
1 teaspoon cinnamon
1/2 teaspoon nutmeg
1/8 teaspoon salt
4 tablespoons butter

Measure one cup of milk and set aside. Heat the remaining milk and then add all other ingredients to it. Cook and stir for 20 minutes until mixture begins to thicken. Pour into a baking dish, and add the remaining milk, but do not stir. Bake for 3 hours without stirring in a 300° oven. Serve warm with cream or ice cream. Serves 8.

DARIOLES AND MAIDS OF HONOUR

Dariole is a French word meaning open pie or tart. Originally it was filled with meat but through the years it was more often made with a cheese or custard filling and it is in variations of this form that the recipe has been handed down to us. One of the earliest receipts for daryols (spelling varies) is included in *The Forme of Cury* compiled about 1390 by the cooks who served Richard II:

"Take creme of cowe milke, (or) almandes. Do thereto ayren (eggs), with sugar, safron, and salt. Medle it ifere (mix it together). Do it in a coffyn of two ynchedepe; bake it wel, and serve it forth."

In the 17ᵗʰ century dainty tarts and pastries became even more popular than they had been, including the now delicately lemon-flavored, custardy dariole.

Such is the power of legend that it is unknown whether darioles were renamed Maids of' Honour for Anne Boleyn and her entourage or to pay homage to Elizabeth I. It is a moot question; different writers make different claims. Evidently both queens and their ladies were particularly fond of them. To further compound the issue, an unnamed linguistic detective has stated that a variation of the word *daryol* meant maid of honour in Chaucer's time so that actually there was no renaming involved, just translating.

The following recipe has been adapted from several that I have collected. I found that the only way to get tart shells that were properly shaped for filling was to bake the dough on the outside of the muffin tin, not in it.

    1 double-crust recipe of pastry
    1/4 pound cream cheese, softened
    3 tablespoons milk
    2 eggs
    1/2 cup sugar
    1/2 cup hot milk
    3 teaspoons lemon-flavored gelatin
    1/2 cup heavy cream, whipped or
    1 cup frozen whipped topping
    Slivered almonds or fruit

Roll out pastry and cut in 12 3-inch rounds, then roll each circle again to thin and stretch it to 4 inches in diameter. With muffin tin upside down, place each circle over a cup and arrange excess fluting as neatly as possible. Bake at 400° for 4 minutes, turn muffin pan end to end, and bake another 4 minutes. Cool slightly before carefully removing to a wire rack.

Soften gelatin in 1/4 cup of water and set aside. Blend cream cheese with 3 tablespoons milk until smooth and free from lumps. Set aside. Beat eggs and sugar in top of double boiler over hot water until they are thick and creamy – a wire whisk works very well. Quickly add hot milk, and cook, stirring constantly. When mixture is custardy in appearance, remove from heat, add gelatin, and blend well. Allow the mixture to cool, then combine with the cream cheese. Lastly, fold in the whipped cream. Fill baked, cooled tart shells, and garnish with slivered almonds or a bit of fruit. Refrigerate till serving time. Makes 12 darioles.

SPRINGTIME SQUARES

Our farm in New Hampshire had a wonderful old row of rhubarb that returned each spring with tender sweet stalks in abundance. When the rhubarb poked up through the thawing ground, we knew that winter's wrath would soon be behind us and the countryside would once again be dressed in all its colorful garb. We knew also that a few servings of rhubarb sauce would be as beneficial as any other spring tonic (and surely taste a good deal better than a dose of cod liver oil!).

This recipe for Springtime Squares is another of those serendipitous finds on a newspaper page of recipes.

For the crust:

1 cup quick oats, uncooked
1/2 cup finely chopped nuts
1/2 cup brown sugar
1/4 cup butter, melted

Line an 8-inch square pan with aluminum foil, extending ends of foil above edge of pan; grease lightly. Combine oats, nuts, and brown sugar with melted butter; mix thoroughly, then press onto bottom of prepared pan. Bake at 375° until light golden brown – about 10 to 12 minutes.

For the filling:

3 cups cut-up rhubarb, fresh or frozen
1 box frozen strawberries, thawed and drained
1 1/4 cups water or orange juice
1 6-ounce package strawberry gelatin
1 cup heavy cream, whipped

Wash and cut rhubarb stalks into 1/2-inch pieces; simmer in water or juice just a few minutes until tender; pour into large bowl and immediately stir in the gelatin and keep stirring until gelatin is dissolved. Add strawberries. Chill about 1 1/2 hours until mixture begins to thicken. Fold whipped cream into rhubarb mixture; carefully spoon onto the crust, letting it mound up, supported by the foil. Chill for 4 hours or more before serving. Serves 9.

APRIL DESIRE

This is a very fancy party dessert that is simple to create. Our grand-mothers would have spent a good deal of time and many egg whites to form the meringues that are an essential part of this recipe. We are more fortunate: we can buy the meringue shells ready to use or substitute a package of soft macaroons, which I found easier to work with and just as tasty.

2 quarts chocolate ice cream, softened
1 dozen macaroons or small meringue shells
1 pint fresh raspberries
2 cups whipped cream
Candied violets
Candied mint leaves

Fill a ring mold with the ice cream, packing it in smoothly; freeze till very firm. Turn out on a chilled circular platter. To do this easily have ready a shallow bowl or pan, filled with boiling water, into which the mold will fit. Hold the mold in the water just long enough to loosen the ice cream, and then flip it on to the serving platter. Press the macaroons on the outside of the ring to make a "fence" around the ice cream. Fill the center of the ring with whipped cream and cover the top of the ice cream with raspberries. Decorate with candied violets and mint leaves for an intriguing presentation.

For the CANDIED FLOWERS and MINT LEAVES you will need superfine sugar, one egg white, and an artist's paintbrush. Beat the egg white in a small bowl until frothy, but not dry; pour some superfine sugar into a shallow bowl. Using the paint brush, coat each flower petal gently with egg white on both sides, then carefully press it into the sugar. Shake off any excess sugar and lay on a waxed paper on a cookie sheet to dry overnight. Candied flowers may be stored for several months if you prepare more than you can use at one time.

Note: not all flowers are suitable for candying, and some blossoms are poisonous so be sure of what you are using. Pansies, violets, lilacs, roses, petunias, and nasturtiums are all edible and make a spectacular addition to any dish, candied or plain.

TO BREAK ONE'S FAST,
OR FOR TIFFIN OR TEA

The recipes in this section can all be served at any time of the day. While most of them are usually thought of as breakfast fare, that does not restrict them to the morning meal. They will work equally well for Tiffin or Tea.

The American Heritage Dictionary defines "tiffin" as a light meal which could be lunch, mid-afternoon tea or supper. "Tea" is strictly a light afternoon interlude, hardly a meal. By contrast, the *Oxford English Dictionary* is more specific and describes "tiffin" as lunch, while "tea" is defined as "a light afternoon meal consisting of tea, bread, cakes, etc." or "a cooked evening meal". "High tea" tends to be even more substantial.

We have all been told over and over about the importance of the first meal of the day; the one that breaks our overnight fast; the one that jump starts the system and gets us ready for the exigencies of the day. It is not surprising, then, to find so many differing recipes for quick breads and egg or cereal dishes. These have come down to us through the years and have become breakfast habit with many of us. Perhaps now is the time to reverse the trend and look at dinner or supper fare that could be served for breakfast just as breakfast items are good any time of the day.

VERMONT THINS

It was logical that Vermonters would substitute maple syrup for sugar as often as they could. They do claim that theirs is the very best maple syrup, though those of us who have lived in other syrup-producing states will dispute that claim.

Early man, in Vermont or elsewhere, did not have a recipe at hand, but he pounded grain and mixed it with a little water and then baked it on a hot rock or directly in the ashes and produced a flat unleavened bread. Generations later we have these delicately flavored pancakes. They can take their place here with Miss Leslie's INDIAN FLAPPERS.

1 cup flour
1 1/2 teaspoons baking powder
Pinch salt
2 tablespoons maple syrup
1 egg
1 cup milk
3 tablespoons melted butter

Stir baking powder and salt into flour. Combine syrup, egg, and milk and add gradually to the flour. Add the melted butter and blend, but do not over beat. Cook on a very hot griddle. Serves 4.

Substitute 2 tablespoons sugar for the maple syrup and add one egg to the above recipe and you will have STRINGS OF FLATS, named for the flatcars that took lumber from forest to market all along the eastern seacoast.

INDIAN FLAPPERS

Eliza Leslie, writing in the mid-1800's, devotes 40 pages of her cookbook to Indian corn and corn meal. She begins the section with two and a half pages of hints on heating ovens and baking in general. She then tells how to make excellent homemade yeast. While her measurements are not specific ("a handful of this, a large spoonful of that"), the recipes are interesting to read just for the details of presentation to the table. Here is her receipt for Indian Flappers:

A quart of sifted Indian meal, a handful of wheat flour, a quart of milk, four eggs, a heaping salt-spoon of salt. Beat the eggs light in another pan, and then stir them a little at a time into the milk, alternately with the meal, a handful at a time. Stir the whole very hard at the last. Have ready a hot griddle, and bake the cakes on it in the manner of buckwheat cakes, or crumpets; greasing or scraping the griddle always before you put on a fresh ladle-full of batter. Make all the cakes the same size, and when done trim the edges nicely with a knife. Send them to table hot, laid one on another evenly, buttered and cut in half. Or they may be buttered after they go to table.

The revised version:

1 cup cornmeal
2 tablespoons flour
1 cup milk
1 egg
Pinch of salt

Beat egg in a small bowl until frothy. Pour milk into a larger bowl and add dry ingredients which have been mixed together alternately with the egg. Stir thoroughly to avoid lumps. The batter will be very thin, but it will thicken slightly if you will let it rest for 10 minutes. Grease a hot griddle with butter, stir batter again, then place small amounts on griddle. Flappers should be no more than 3 inches in diameter. Turn once. Serve with maple or blueberry syrup. Serves 3.

POPOVERS

If you are lucky enough to have a cast iron gem pan, you will certainly want to make this delicate bread with some frequency. If, like most folks, you only have a regular muffin pan, make them anyway. They will be just as good – well, almost.

1 cup flour
Pinch of salt
2 eggs
1 cup milk
1 tablespoon melted butter

Grease iron gem pans or muffin tins and preheat in oven while you are mixing the batter. Combine all ingredients in a deep bowl and beat with a rotary beater until smooth. Fill the hot pans no more than half full. Bake in a 425° oven for 35 minutes. Do not open oven door to peek or they will not be popped. Serve hot with additional butter. Makes 12 popovers.

As a variation, try INDIAN PUFFS. Use 1/2 cup flour and 1/2 cup corn meal in place of the 1 cup flour. The method is the same as above.

Or you could follow Miss Leslie's suggestion and make SUNDER-LANDS. Make a small slit in the side of each popover and with a teaspoon very gently fill the cavity with marmalade or jam.

Gem Pan

YANKEE GEMS

While perusing *The American Heritage Cookbook,* I noticed a recipe for Graham Gems neatly tucked between various muffin recipes. I spent quite a bit of time, then, trying to find the origin of the word *gem* as it refers to a small bread or cake, but with little success. If the basic ingredients and proportions are the same why is one called a gem and the other a muffin?

The only thing I determined for certain is that *gem* is an old-fashioned American term and its use probably depended on whether the dough was baked in a cast iron gem pan or a muffin tin.

The following recipe for a gem with a hidden ingredient is typical of New England cooking. It is adapted from Allan Keller's *Grandma's Cooking.*

2 cups flour
1 teaspoon cinnamon
1/4 teaspoon ginger
1/4 teaspoon nutmeg
1/4 teaspoon salt
1 teaspoon baking soda
2 tablespoons brown sugar
1/3 cup butter, melted
3/4 cup molasses
1 egg
1 1/2 tablespoons milk
1/2 cup currants or raisins
1 apple

Sift dry ingredients together into large bowl; add melted butter and molasses and mix well. Beat egg with milk and add to mixture, then add currants or raisins as desired. Peel and core apple. Cut into small chunks and place several in each cup of a <u>well-greased</u> muffin tin or gem pan if you have one. Spoon dough over apple chunks and bake at 350° for 25 to 30 minutes. Makes 12 medium muffins.

LAPLANDS AND BOUNCING BABIES

This is a richer and slightly more elaborate version of the recipe for Popovers. Beating the egg whites separately from the other ingredients adds more air to the mixture, then, in the heat of the oven, the air expands until you have an empty cavity just waiting to be filled with butter and jam.

Add a tablespoon of sugar to the batter and dust the tops with more sugar as they come from the oven and you will have BOUNCING BABIES to serve as a dessert filled with fruit preserves. Or elaborate even more and fill the cavities with custard or whipped cream and you will have made CREAM PUFFS. Use your imagination or see the recipe for DUTCH BABIES, which gives another variation.

3 eggs, separated
1 cup flour
1 cup milk
1 tablespoon melted butter
Salt to taste

Grease and flour muffin tins and place in oven to heat while you are preparing the batter. In a medium-sized bowl blend the egg yolks, flour, milk, and melted butter using a rotary beater or electric blender. Mixture should be smooth and free of lumps. Fold in stiffly beaten egg whites. Pour batter into greased, floured, and heated muffin tins, filling them no more than half full. Bake at 375° for 35 to 40 minutes. Laplands should be well puffed up and delicately browned. Makes 12.

WIGS

"And we had the most delightful things for tea and some things – cakes – Mrs. Wishart calls wigs, the best things you ever saw in your life." (Susan Werner, *Nobody,* 1832)

Wigs or Whigs were first mentioned in the 14th century. They were baked in one large pan and cut into wedges, hence the name which derives from *wigge,* meaning wedge. Originally made with yeast and spices, wigs have been altered through the years as the ingredients and baking instructions were changed. Here is the recipe that William Penn's wife, Gulielma, used:

Take half peck of flouer by measure, then a pound of butter and breke it ino it with youre hands; the quantity of an ounce: of nutmegs, mace and sinomen together in fine pouder; three quarters of a pound of Caraway comfits, a pint and a half of yeist, the same of milk, it must be blood warme, be sure you do not over bake them. [Caraway comfits are sugar-coated caraway seeds.]

A recipe for "whigs, 1900, as made by Mrs. Stubbs, near Loughborough" is given in *Food in England.* Here is a scaled-down version of it.

2 cups flour
1 tablespoon sugar
1 teaspoon baking powder
Pinch of salt
1 teaspoon lemon peel
1 egg
1 cup milk
3 tablespoons butter, melted
1/4 cup currants, raisins, or dried cranberries

Mix together the dry ingredients. In a large bowl, whisk the egg vigorously; add the milk and melted butter. Add the flour and currants or other dried fruit and stir just enough to moisten the flour. Spoon batter into a greased 9-inch pie pan and spread out evenly. Bake at 400° for 20 minutes. Cut into 8 wedges.

Or you may bake the wigs in greased muffin cups as Mrs. Stubbs directed since they are neither scones nor muffins, but somewhere in between.

NANTUCKET WONDERS, BUTTERFLY WINGS AND DUTCHMAN'S BREECHES

When is a doughnut not a doughnut, or even a cruller? When it is a Wonder, of course! Though a member of the doughnut family by virtue of being fried in deep fat, a Wonder is more like a cookie in texture and consistency, but not as sweet.

References to Wonders in cookbooks are few and far between, but the name appears to be indigenous to Nantucket Island. In *Treasury of New England Folklore,* R.A. Botkin mentions Wonders and quotes from a memoir of life on Nantucket Island by Joseph E.C.Farnham:

"Surely the Wonder was - may I say so? - the king of doughnuts . . crisp, deliciously browned . . . and peculiarly appetizing."

My introduction to Wonders came as I was perusing my very battered copy of *Miss Leslie's New Receipts for Cooking.* According to Miss Leslie (and Mr. Farnham), a jagging iron or jagger knife was requisite to making a proper Wonder. These were originally made of ivory, beautifully shaped and intricately carved as in the manner of scrimshaw. They consisted of a handle about four or five inches long with a wheel about an inch in diameter fitted into one end. The edge of the wheel was carved to give a jagged line when cutting the dough. Modern-day pastry wheels are descendents of jagging irons. But don't rush to the nearest antique shop to buy a jagging iron - unless you are a purist. Very fine Wonders can be made using an ordinary table knife.

1/2 cup margarine or shortening
2 1/2 cups flour
3/4 cup sugar
1/2 teaspoon cinnamon
1/2 teaspoon salt
1/4 cup white wine, water, or fruit juice
3 eggs
Vegetable oil for frying

Cut margarine or shortening into flour in mixing bowl, using two table knives or a pastry blender. Then rub together with hands until no lumps of shortening remain. Mixture should resemble corn meal. Add sugar, cinnamon, and salt and stir to mix. Add wine, water or juice, and mix well. Beat eggs very well with a rotary beater and add to mixture, blending in thoroughly. If necessary, add a bit more flour – dough should be fairly stiff. Roll out on floured board to quarter-inch thickness.

Cut with plain round cutter (2 to 3 inches in diameter). With jagging iron or table knife make one cut through each circle along the diameter, but not all the way through to the edges. Make two more short cuts, one on each side of the long one. Have ready deep fat heated to 375° and fry Wonders, a few at a time, until nicely browned. Turn once during frying. If the fat is at the proper temperature, they will be done in 3 to 4 minutes. Drain on absorbent paper. Dust with powdered sugar if you like. This will make a 12 or more Wonders, depending upon the size of your cutter.

For BUTTERFLY WINGS, roll the dough as thinly as you can, then cut into 1 1/2x4 inch strips. Cut a lengthwise slit in each strip; pass one end of the strip through the slit, forming a knot. Fry as for Wonders.

For DUTCHMAN'S BREETCHES, cut rolled dough into 3-inch squares. Make a cut on one side halfway through to center. As they cook, they will swell on each side of the cut to resemble a little boy's short pants.

Or you could just make OLYKOEKS – that is what the citizens of Nieuw Amsterdam called doughnuts. Then you could share speculation on why there is a hole in the center. One story suggests that a sea captain ordered them that way so that he could hang them on the spokes of his steering wheel where they would always be handy. Another tale is that a Pilgrim mother was frying cakes one day when an Indian appeared at the kitchen window and shot an arrow right through the middle of one. The sensible answer, of course, is so that the doughnuts will be completely cooked.

Jagging Iron

HANGTOWN FRY

In the early days of the Gold Rush, two miners took $17,000 worth of gold dust from a place called Old Dry Diggings, near the site of Sutter's Mill. A year later the first recorded execution for murder in the gold region took place at Old Dry Diggings and the name was promptly changed to Hangtown. The town grew rapidly and gradually became more genteel until once again a name change was in order. It is known today as Placerville.

A story from those early days of the Gold Rush tells of a hungry miner who stumbled out of the hills and into the first saloon he saw in rough and boisterous Hangtown. Throwing his poke on the bar, he demanded that he be served the most expensive food in town. At that time, in that place, hen's eggs and oysters from the Pacific Ocean were the two costliest items available. Luckily, the saloon keeper just happened to have both at hand and quickly stirred up a dish of Hangtown Fry.

1 dozen oysters
8 eggs
Butter or margarine
Salt and pepper to taste

Wash the oysters, pat dry with paper towel, and chop or cut into several pieces. Sauté them gently for a few minutes in a large frying pan. Stir eggs together with salt and pepper and pour over oysters. Scramble all together till done. Serves 4 – or one hungry miner.

KENTUCKY SCRAMBLE

The corn in this scrambled egg recipe gives a distinctly different flavor and texture. It is a good way to use any leftover fresh corn cut from the cob, but frozen or canned corn will work as well. If you have bacon drippings, do use them; they enhance the flavor of the scramble. The recipe is adapted from the *American Heritage Cookbook.*

1 1/2 cups cooked corn
1 medium green pepper, chopped
1 teaspoon chopped fresh parsley or 1/2 teaspoon dried
2 slices pimiento, chopped
8 eggs
Salt and pepper to taste
3 to 4 tablespoons bacon drippings or butter

Heat bacon drippings or butter in large skillet. Add drained corn and sauté gently for a few minutes. Stir in the pepper, parsley, and pimiento and cook for 5 or 6 minutes.

Beat eggs in bowl with salt and pepper, if desired, pour over corn mixture, and scramble all together. Serve with crisp bacon strips to 6 for breakfast or lunch.

WELSH RABBIT, GOLDEN BUCK, AND MORE

Can you imagine the terrible embarrassment you would feel if you had invited 50 or more people to dinner and suddenly found there was not enough to serve everyone? The story goes that a certain Welsh chieftain found himself in just such a predicament and rather than be humiliated in front of his guests, he ordered his cooks to produce something – anything – so that no one would know that the supply of game was so limited. Quick, imaginative thinking produced a melted mixture of cheese and beer that was poured directly over a trencher of bread. In honor of his master and to preserve his prestige, the cook named this new dish Welsh Rabbit.

Possibly this is the way Welsh Rabbit, or rarebit, was created, but I believe it is more likely to assume that it was a poor man's dish that was given a fancy title. In the olden days in England and Wales, game of any kind was only rarely available to the peasants. Hunting in the large forests and huge game preserves was the exclusive privilege of the rich. A poor man was much more apt to have cheese on hand than rabbit or any other meat, and one can easily imagine him being facetious or perhaps envious and calling it Welsh Rabbit.

Linguistically, there is no basis for the word "rarebit", although it is the term found in most cookbooks. It is probable that it was coined by a restaurant menu writer whose task it was to glorify each dish and never present any food in simple terms. I wonder if the same writer was responsible for names like Golden Buck, Rinktum Tiddy, or Brer Rabbit in the Cornpatch – all names for variations of Welsh Rabbit. No matter what you call it, this is a good dish to remember when you want to serve something that can be prepared quickly and easily and that is not too filling. It makes a good luncheon dish or an after-outing supper.

1 pound grated cheddar cheese
1 cup milk or beer
3 eggs
2 teaspoons Worcestershire sauce
2 teaspoons butter
1 teaspoon dry mustard
Dash cayenne pepper
Salt and pepper to taste

Combine all ingredients in a saucepan and stir over low heat until the cheese melts and the mixture is perfectly smooth. Do not allow to boil. Serve immediately over toast triangles in a soup plate. Serves 6.

GOLDEN BUCK is Welsh Rabbit topped with a freshly poached egg. RINKTUM TIDDY, RUM TUM TIDDY, or RUM TUM-DITTY (take your pick) are variations of Welsh Rabbit made with undiluted condensed tomato soup in place of the milk or beer. Suggested garnishes are crumbled bacon, small sausages, ham strips, or pickle slices. This dish is also known as PINK BUNNY.

For a heartier version try BRER RABBIT IN THE CORNPATCH. To a recipe of Pink Bunny add 1 cup whole kernel corn. Place a slice of ham on a piece of toast and pour the cheese-corn mixture over it. Serve with salad and a dessert, and it becomes a very acceptable supper for a hot summer's night.

ENGLISH MONKEY

As a new bride, I relied on one wedding present almost daily. *Good Cooking Made Easy* became my "Bible" as I learned how to use the pots and pans and varied kitchen equipment that I found in our rented apartment. I don't believe the English had anything to do with this mixture of milk and melted cheese; the authors made no comment on the name. However, it soon became a favorite for a quick Sunday night supper. It reminded me of the Milk Toast my grandmother fixed for me as a youngster. That was comfort food and so is English Monkey.

1 cup milk
1 cup dry bread crumbs
1 tablespoon butter
Salt and pepper to taste
1 cup grated cheddar cheese
1 egg
4 slices toast

Scald the milk in the top of a double boiler; add the bread crumbs, butter, and salt and pepper if desired. Add the cheese and stir over hot water until cheese has melted and mixture is well blended. Stir in the slightly beaten egg; cook for another minute or two. Pour over toast. Makes 4 servings

TOAD-IN-THE-HOLE

Toad-in-the-Hole is a recipe of English origin. While most recipes call for small sausages such as our breakfast links, frankfurters may be substituted.

2 pounds link sausage or frankfurters
1 cup flour
1/4 teaspoon salt
2 eggs
1 cup milk
4 tablespoons butter or margarine
4 tablespoons flour
1/4 teaspoon dry mustard
2 cups milk
1 cup American or cheddar cheese, cut up or grated

Simmer sausages or frankfurters in water while preparing batter, in order to get them heated through. Put flour and salt in small, deep mixing bowl; add eggs and milk and beat with a rotary beater till well blended. Place sausage, or frankfurters cut in half, in lightly greased 9x13-inch baking dish. Leave space between them. Pour batter over them and bake in 400° oven for 30 minutes. Batter should be puffed up and golden.

Meanwhile, prepare cheese sauce by blending butter and flour in saucepan, allowing them to bubble together for at least a minute. Stir constantly. Remove from heat, add mustard and salt and pepper to taste. Add milk and cheese and return to heat; stir until thickened over medium heat. Pour cheese sauce over Toad-in-the-Hole when it comes from the oven or serve separately at the table. Serves 4 to 6.

TO QUENCH ONE'S THIRST

If all be true that I do think,
There are five reasons that we should drink;
Good wine – a friend – or being dry –
Or lest we should be by and by –
Or any other reason why.

We all need to drink, especially water; we cannot survive more than four days without it. A good supply of clean, fresh, palatable water has been a priority from man's first days on earth. Of course, problems developed as the population grew and spread out. To meet the need to move water from its source to areas where people were living, pipes or conduits were carved out of wood, clay, or stone, relying on gravity for the flow. Some were very simple, but as cities began to grow, the systems became more elaborate. The Roman aqueducts, some of which are still in use today, are notable examples.

Getting water to the people was only one part of the problem. Another was how to cope with the recurring plagues that ravaged closely settled areas. Many people suffered unusual gastric pains or died of unknown diseases. It was not until the middle of the 1800s that a connection was finally made between unclean, contaminated water and the spread of disease. Much has been done since then to ensure that our tap water is clean, fresh, and palatable.

We must forgive Henry Aldrich for recommending wine instead of water. He wrote the ditty above sometime during the latter half of the 17th century, perhaps while the second London plague was devastating the city. Wine would have been his drink of choice, and it would not have occurred to him to think of water in its place. But his philosophy is good: we need to drink, if not water, then one of the beverages offered here.

HAYMAKER'S SWITCHEL

Haying season is an indefinite time in the summer when the weather has been just right, the grass is high, and the farmer is of a mind to mow. Even with modern equipment it is hot, tiring work; with a scythe, as haying was done in early days, it was even more demanding. It fell to the early housewife to provide a thirst-quenching, morale-boosting, refreshing drink. Since berries and other fruits used for juice were seasonal and citrus fruits were rare treats, Switchel was made from ingredients more readily at hand.

1 cup brown sugar
1/2 cup molasses
2 quarts water
1/2 cup cider vinegar
1/2 teaspoon ginger

Mix all ingredients together, being sure that sugar is dissolved. Chill. This is a sweet-tart drink that is very different from the fruity drinks to which we are more accustomed. It may not be to everyone's liking.

CIRCUS FREEZE

Here is a colorful and refreshing drink that is just right for one of the dog days of summer. The contrasting flavors complement each other nicely.

For each person fill a tall glass with crushed ice.

Pour into a glass 1/8 cup each of

Orange juice
Raspberry juice
Lime juice
Loganberry juice

Pour very slowly and carefully so that the juices are layered, not mixed. Serve with a colored straw. Cranberry juice may be substituted for the loganberry juice, which might be hard to find.

GOLD STRIKE

Years ago when my children gave me a case of mumps that caused great difficulty in swallowing, I drank at least one eggnog every day. That was before I learned that raw eggs are known to be a boost to the immune system and provide balanced nutrition while also being easy to swallow and digest. It was also before we had to worry about where our eggs came from or their freshness. I have included this recipe because a well-made eggnog can be the best medicine sometimes, but *please, please be sure the eggs you use are clean and fresh and you know that they come from a reputable farm.*

For each serving beat or shake together until frothy:

1 cup chilled orange juice
1 tablespoon honey
1 egg

Pour into a tall glass, garnish with a snippet of fruit or an edible flower – pansy, nasturtium or marigold – and serve at once.

WINTER GROG

After a cold winter's day on the snow-covered slopes of New Hampshire, we welcomed this spicy drink that warmed our insides as we vied for positions near the big wood-burning kitchen stove. The spices and the orange peel give the coffee an extra zing.

6 cups (48 ounces) hot coffee
1/4 teaspoon ground cardamom
1 small stick cinnamon
1/8 teaspoon allspice
Sugar to taste
Peel of one orange
Whipped cream (optional)

Combine all ingredients except the whipped cream and stir thoroughly. Keep warm but not boiling and allow to steep for 15 minutes. Remove cinnamon stick and orange peel and serve with whipped cream as desired. Serves 8 to 10.
The spices and citrus flavor work equally well with cocoa, hot chocolate, or tea.

BIBLIOGRAPHY

Allen, Ida Bailey. *The Modern Method Of Preparing Delightful Foods.*
New York: Corn Products Refining Co. (No Date)

Brown, Alice Cooke. *Early American Herb Recipes.*
New York: Bonanza Books, 1966.

Cannon, Poppy And Brooks, Patricia. *The Presidents' Cookbook.*
New York: Bonanza Books, 1968.

Carlton, Jan McBride. *The Old-Fashioned Cookbook.*
New York: Holt, Rinehart and Winston, 1975.

Farmer, Fannie Merritt. *The Boston Cooking School Cookbook.*
Boston: Little Brown And Co., 1934.

Gilbreth, Frank Jr. *Of Whales and Women.*

Gould, John. *Monstrous Depravity.*
New York: William Morrow And Co., 1963.

Hartley, Dorothy. *Food in England.*
London: Macdonald And Co., 1969.

Havighurst, Walter. *The Heartland: Oh, In, Il.*
New York: Harper and Row, 1956.

Heseltine, Marjorie and Dow, Ula M. *Good Cooking.*
New York: Houghton and Mifflin Co., 1936.

Home Institute of New York Herald Tribune, *America's Cook Book.*
New York: Charles Scribner's Sons, 1938.

Jackson, Joseph Henry, Ed. *Gold Rush Album.*
New York: Charles Scribner's Sons, 1949.

Keller, Allan. *Grandma's Cooking.*
New York: Gramercy Publishing Co., 1955.

Leslie, Miss Eliza. *New Receipts for Cooking.*
Philadelphia: T.R. Peterson, 1854.

Lord, Isabel Ely, (Ed.) *Everybody's Cook Book.*
New York: Harcourt, Brace Co., 1924.

Macdonald, Duncan and Sagendorph, Robb. *Rain, Hail And Baked Beans.*
New York: Ives Washburn, Inc., 1958.

Mosser, Marjorie. *Foods of Old New England.*
New York: Doubleday, 1957.

Mrs. Beeton's Cookery and Household Management.
London: Ward, Lock And Co., Ltd., 1960.

Rohde, Eleanour Sinclair. *A Garden Of Herbs.*
Boston and New York: Hale, Cushman and Flint, 1936.

Rorer, Mrs. S. T. *Hot Weather Dishes.*
Philadelphia: Arnold And Co., 1888.

Sagendorph, Robb. *America and Her Almanacs.*
Boston: Little, Brown & Co., 1970.

Stover, Blanche M. *Parent's Magazine Family Cookbook.*
New York: Mcgraw, Hill Book Co. Inc., 1953.

Taber, Gladys. *My Own Cookbook.*
Philadelphia, New York: J. P. Lippincott Co., 1972.

Tannahill, Reay. *Food in History.*
New York: Stein And Day, 1974.

The American Heritage Cookbook.
American Heritage Publishing Co. Inc., 1964.

Trager, James. *The Food Book.*
New York: Avon Books, 1972.

Truax, Carol, Ed. *Ladies Home Journal Dessert Cookbook.*
New York: Doubleday And Co., 1964.

Wolcott, Imogene. *The New England Yankee Cookbook.*
New York: Coward-McCann, 1939.

INDEX